EFFECT OF AGE AND EXPERIENCE
ON TESTS OF INTELLIGENCE

BY

VERNON A. JONES, Ph.D.

TEACHERS COLLEGE, COLUMBIA UNIVERSITY
CONTRIBUTIONS TO EDUCATION, NO. 203

BUREAU OF PUBLICATIONS
Teachers College, Columbia University
NEW YORK CITY
1926

Library of Congress Cataloging in Publication Data

Jones, Vernon Augustus, 1897-
   Effect of age and experience on tests of intelligence.

   Reprint of the 1926 ed., issued in series: Teachers
College, Columbia University. Contributions to edu-
cation, no. 203.
   Originally presented as the author's thesis, Columbia.
   Bibliography: p.
   1. Mental tests. 2. Age and intelligence.
3. Experience. I. Title. II. Series: Columbia
University. Teachers College. Contributions to edu-
cation, no. 203.
BF431.J635 1972   153.9'32   75-176919
ISBN 0-404-55203-X

Reprinted by Special Arrangement with Teachers
College Press, New York, New York

From the edition of 1926 , New York
First AMS edition published in 1972
Manufactured in the United States

AMS PRESS, INC.
NEW YORK, N. Y.   10003

ACKNOWLEDGMENTS

EVERY study conducted in that realm of educational psychology known as tests and measurements must be a coöperative study. Even if we can conceive of one's being so capable that he is not forced to call upon others at any time for aid in deciding upon techniques and methods of procedure, he is, by the very nature of the field in which he is working, compelled to receive assistance from many boys and girls who act as subjects for the experiment. I wish, therefore, first to mention the four hundred and eighty-seven children who, taken as a group, worked for at least eight hundred hours on the tests with which this study deals. Other uses were made of the results in the case of every child, but even though these children did not work for this length of time especially for the sake of this experiment, the study would have been impossible without their enormous contribution.

Second, I am very grateful to the superintendents and principals of schools from which the original data were obtained for their cordial coöperation. Special mention should be made of the following: Mr. Herman Gress, former Superintendent of Schools, Monessen, Pa.; Mr. Albert H. Hill, Superintendent of Schools, Richmond, Va.; Miss Abby P. Leland, Principal of Public School Number 1, Bronx, New York City; Miss Harriet O'Shea, Principal of Children's University School, New York City; Mr. Morton Snyder, Principal of Scarboro School, Scarboro-on-Hudson, N. Y.

For inspiration and valuable suggestions in connection with the problem, I am particularly indebted to Professor Godfrey H. Thomson, of Armstrong College, University of Durham, Newcastle-upon-Tyne, England, and formerly Visiting Professor in Teachers College, Columbia University; and to Professors Rudolf Pintner, William A. McCall, and J. Ralph McGaughy of Teachers College, Columbia University.

V. A. J.

CONTENTS

TABLES

FIGURES

EFFECT OF AGE AND EXPERIENCE ON TESTS OF INTELLIGENCE

CHAPTER I

THE PROBLEM DEFINED

As a by-product of a previous study (1924) [1] it was noticed that a score on one sub-test [2] of an intelligence examination may depend more exclusively on native brightness than scores on other sub-tests. The fact observed was not new, but the particular circumstances in which it was observed have led to what is believed to be a new attack. Suppose we are dealing with two pupils, A and B, for whom the following relationships hold:

Pupil A		*Pupil B*
Mental Age	=	Mental Age
Chronological Age	<	Chronological Age

But it was found that

Score on sub-test X	>	Score on sub-test X

Some sub-test must exist where

Score on sub-test Y	<	Score on sub-test Y

Otherwise the two mental ages could not be equal.

On intelligence tests, as constructed at present, a young bright child and an old dull child obtain their mental age ratings by performance on the same sub-tests. It would seem that any sub-test that depends upon the bare fact of living in the world—sub-test Y for instance—would favor the dull child. Thus if we find that some sub-test is tending less towards measuring native brightness than the whole battery and is depending more on chronological age than the battery, we may question, so far as this sub-test's contri-

---

[1] In the Bibliography, pp. 73 to 74, will be found the complete reference which is here indicated by date. This arrangement has been followed throughout the study.

[2] By sub-test is meant a type of situation presented to the subject; for example, in the Binet-Simon Test the 'repeating of digits' or the 'detecting of absurdities in passage read', or in group tests, 'arithmetic problems', or 'analogies'.

bution is concerned, whether a mental age of eight for an eleven-year-old child means the same thing as a mental age of eight for a seven-year-old child.

If changes in a sub-test score are related to changes in chronological age (C.A.), this may mean, to the extent of the relationship, dependence strictly on length of life; but abilities depending on C.A. may be interpreted as depending either on greater opportunity to learn, due to length of life, or on greater opportunity to learn, due to better environment or more careful supervision on the part of elders. Provided a satisfactory technique can be discovered for showing the above, we can evaluate various sub-tests on the basis of whether each is tending more or less than the battery to measure native brightness relatively free from the effects of mere living in the world and from the effects of environmental conditions. It is obvious that this may lead to a consideration of whether the mental ages as indicated by the entire battery may not be leaning too much in one direction or the other, and this very question would be tending toward a new definition of mental age. This last consideration, however, would be beyond the bounds of this study.

For the sake of clarity, we have spoken up to this point somewhat as if the problem were simply a matter of determining how much each sub-test depended on C.A. Certainly, however, the case is not so simple. A sub-test may not depend at all upon C.A. and yet be a poor one because it does not measure mental age (M.A.). In order to determine which sub-tests are good for a battery, we wish to know how well the scores on these differentiate between the brighter and the duller children of the same chronological age. But we want to know, in addition, what relations exist between scores on the sub-tests and chronological ages for children who are of the same mental maturity. We desire sub-tests which show high positive correlation with M.A. for children who are alike in C.A.; for children who are alike in M.A. we desire tests which show no relation to C.A. These are two different demands, and are not two ways of saying the same thing. A sub-test may correlate with the best obtainable mental ages to the extent of $+.70$ for a group alike in C.A. and similar in environmental circumstances, and so far it might appear to be one of our best sub-tests. But since it is not correlating perfectly with mental age, we do not know what will happen if it is given a chance to measure changes in C.A. and in environmental conditions, these two being free to vary. It is even easier to see that a sub-test which satisfies the condition of not correlating with C.A. is not necessarily a good one, because it may prove good from this one viewpoint and yet not measure mental age at all.

One other complexity suggests itself. Where will be obtained the measures of mental maturity which are to be used as a part of the criterion? If the sub-tests are to be tested on the basis of how well they measure mental maturity stripped of all traces of C.A., this demands not only a method for doing it but also some pure mental measures to start with. Such measures are not available. Two alternatives face us. The first is to give up because we do not have a satisfactory measure to use as a basis. This suggests an interesting line of thought which has formed the starting point for sundry different types of destructive arguments. It is something like this: If we do not have an entirely satisfactory measure with which to start, we cannot prove anything; if the measure is satisfactory, there is nothing to prove. A second attitude which might be taken is to begin with the best knowledge available. Applied to the problem at hand this would mean the use of some of the best measures of mental maturity that are obtainable. Though it is thought that these measures will be imperfect as a result of depending upon sub-tests which measure to varying degrees factors irrelevant to brightness, the sub-tests which are most guilty of this defect may be discovered. Once they are discovered, they may be eliminated, and through the use of those remaining, new measures—not perfect but better ones— will result.

The steps outlined in the latter part of the preceding paragraph represent the writer's idea as to how the results of such a study as this may be applied toward the improvement of mental ages. They do not represent an outline of what is to be attempted here. The proposal in this study is to take the first step, that is, to evaluate sub-tests on the basis of which depend most on factors that apparently have little to do with mental endowment. In other words, this article will confine itself to the problem of the effect of age and experience on certain component tests of some widely used group examinations. Not only does it appear that the steps given above are necessary to obtain a better mental age by the attack that is here proposed, but it would seem that the *order* of the steps is logical. Specifically, it appears that once we have decided upon mental ages that are to be taken as a part of the criterion, we cannot move up to the second step and try to make the criterion better until we have compared every sub-test with the original one accepted. With the admission that the mental ages in the criterion are not perfect measures but the best that it was feasible to obtain, we shall proceed as if the mental ages were perfect measures, and we shall confine ourselves to the first step. If it is found that some sub-tests are subject to the influence of age and environmental conditions more than others, on the basis of our criterion, we shall be content in this study to point out this fact and to indicate briefly as we go along its implication on the theory and technique of mental measurement. The problem of eliminating those sub-tests found to be most undesirable, or— what amounts to the same thing—the construction of an examination which includes only those sub-tests which appear best according to our criterion, will not be attempted here. And obviously we cannot take the third step of getting new and better measures without having taken the second. In confining ourselves to the first part of the process, however, we shall not be barred from a theoretical view of the outcome.

Though the method of attack employed here is different from that used elsewhere, and though no one has dealt with this matter in much detail in the field of group tests, the general problem of this study is an old one, and one which has received attention from many writers.

Stern (1912) says: "There are certain abilities that are essentially a function of age, relatively independent of intelligence; there are other abilities that are conditioned entirely by specific degrees of intellectual development, regardless of the age at which this development is attained. . . . It will be of great value for us to be able to discover by analysis of the results of Binet-Simon Tests which of the tests applied to the feeble-minded correlate more with age and which more with real intelligence."

Comparing the results of Chotzen on feebleminded children of eight and nine years and the results of Bobertag on normal children of the same ages, Stern concludes that the backwardness of the feebleminded was least in the following tests: 'telling forenoon from afternoon', 'defining in terms of use', 'knowing one's own age', 'esthetic judgment', 'telling the number of fingers', 'describing a picture', 'counting thirteen pennies'. The backwardness was, on the other hand, very pronounced in the following: 'memory-span for sixteen syllables', 'memory-span for five digits', 'making change', 'counting backwards from twenty to zero', 'definition of superordinate terms', 'comparison of two objects from memory', 'recall of a short story', 'naming the months', 'arranging of five weights'.

Meumann (1913), in adapting the Binet-Simon Tests for use in Hamburg, proposed a division of tests at each age level into three separate divisions, viz., tests of development or **maturity**, tests of intelligence, and tests of environment. To give some idea of his divisions, the tests at the ten-year level are reproduced here.

Tests of Development	Tests of Intelligence	Tests of Environment
6. Repetitions of four to six letters or digits and sentences up to 40 syllables.	3. Making sentences containing 3 or 2 words. 4. Comprehension questions. 8. Fables tests.	1. Time orientation. (Naming the months, seasons in which Easter, Pentecost, and X'mas come, etc.)
9. Suggestion, with lines.		2. Knowledge of coins, paper money, post-marks, address, time-tables.
10. Esthetic judg-ment,		5. Space. The unfolding experiment, copying a drawing.
a. Of simple pictures. b. Of different artistic pictures. c. Of ugly objects and pictures.		7. Vocabulary test.

The point to be emphasized is not which sub-tests Meumann selected for each division—for this is open to some discussion—but the fact that he felt all the sub-tests were not equally immune from the effects of development and environment.

Claparede (1914), who comments at length on Meumann's series, makes the following significant statement: "If we discover that a function is in close relation to a certain age level, new investigations will be necessary to tell us whether the execution of the test depends on age itself, that is to say, on certain degrees of maturity of the brain or the mind, or whether age has only intervened indirectly by multiplying opportunities of exercise of the function. . . ."

Terman and Childs in 1912, during the time that they were making the Stanford Revision of the Binet Test, which has proved to be such a valuable contribution to mental measurement in this country, made the following statement about the theory underlying the selection of sub-tests: "The only way to make sure that our measurement will arrive at any approximation of the former (i.e., a measure of intelligence) is to choose for our tests types of performance which will not be too greatly influenced by such differences in training and experience as ordinarily exist among the children of civilized people living under fairly uniform conditions of home life and educational advantages."

Pintner and Patterson (1914) gave an example of two sub-tests used in the Binet-Simon Tests which appeared to them to depend too much upon experience. These were (1) 'the naming of the days of the week', and (2) 'the naming of the months of the year'.[1] Their results are based on an examination of 988 persons in institutions for the feebleminded, of whom 382 were below fifteen years and 606 above fifteen years in chronological age. The following sentences are taken from their report: "For the *days test* at age six we now have 80% passes as compared with 59% for the younger children. . . . The point seems to be that it is experience alone and not mental ability that is shown. The inability of a child of nine or ten to pass these two tests does not preclude him from being able to pass them at a later date notwithstanding permanent mental arrest." The fact that the two sub-tests which are emphasized above happen to be alternates in the Stanford Revision of the Binet Scale does not detract from the point that is being made by the authors relative to the influence of C.A. on sub-test scores, because the same criticism has been made of two of the tests that are not alternates, by Dr. Taylor (1923). Referring to the 'naming of coins', she says: "It was believed that merely years of living, of experiencing years of life, affected the test (Stanford Revision of the Binet) results." At another place in this thesis she criticizes from the same angle the sub-test 'counting backwards from twenty to zero'.

Though statements could be taken from the writings of several others [2] to show the seriousness with which this problem (i.e., the

---

[1] The former is used as an alternate test in the Stanford Revision at age seven; the latter is an alternate at age nine. In the original Binet-Simon Scale the former was included in the 1908 Scale, but omitted in the 1911 Revision, while the latter appeared in both 1908 and 1911.

[2] In addition to the authors quoted, I have been assisted especially by the writings of Bickersteth, Chapman and Dale, Gordon, and Ruml.

dependence of sub-tests on factors other than brightness) has been considered, only one other quotation will be included. Whipple (1924), who seems to have given a great deal of attention to this problem and has seen fit to translate into English many foreign comments upon it, may well be chosen to summarize the point. He does it in one sentence. He says: "Generally speaking, it would seem desirable to exclude from our intelligence examinations any test that exhibited marked correlations with chronological age, coupled with low correlation with endowment."

CHAPTER II

THE DATA AND THE METHOD OF PROCEDURE

Mental ages were obtained by means of four group intelligence tests for 487 school children taken from four different towns or cities. Table I shows the distribution of these pupils by schools and by school grades. The mental age for each child was determined by getting a median of the four mental ages obtained by the four examinations. Then each sub-test of the examinations was correlated, by partial correlation methods, against mental age and against chronological age. A twofold criterion was set up, and the sub-tests were ranked on the basis of how near they approached this.

TABLE I

DISTRIBUTION OF 487 PUPILS BY SCHOOLS AND GRADES

Schools	School Grades							Grand Total
	7th	6th	5th	Total	4th	3rd	Total	
Children's University School, New York City	I	6	14	21	23	9	32	53
Monessen, Pa.	..	28	24	52	34	20	54	106
Public School No. 1, Bronx, New York City	..	59	20	79	..	..	..	79
Scarboro, N. Y.....	..	13	14	27	14	..	14	41
Richmond, Va.	..	..	208	208	..	..	..	208
Totals	I	106	280	387	71	29	100	487

The Tests.—The four tests selected were: National Intelligence Test, Scale A; National Intelligence Test, Scale B; Haggerty Intelligence Examination, Delta 2; Otis Group Intelligence Scale, Advanced Examination. This battery was given to only 387 children. One hundred pupils in this study were in the third and fourth grades, and for this group the battery was not exactly the same as above, the Otis Primary Examination being substituted for the Advanced in these lower grades.

There were several reasons for the selection of these particular tests. First, they were very carefully standardized, each being the product of one or more of America's most eminent specialists in test construction. Second, in all studies where group test results have been compared with results on batteries composed of other group tests or with Binet Mental ages, these four rank among the best. The figures reported by Gates, Stenquist, and Root are representative. Gates and Root worked the correlations between Stanford-Binet mental ages and mental ages of several group tests. The former (1922) reports the following results:

Tests	r	σ
National Test, Scale A	.47	.05
National Test, Scale B	.45	.04
Haggerty Test, Delta 2	.48	.17
Otis Advanced Examination	.61	.06
Dearborn, Test 4	.52	.17
Dearborn, Test 5	.49	.05
Dearborn, 4 and 5 combined	.58	.09
Illinois I	.45	.12

Root (1922) reports the correlations between Stanford-Binet mental ages and group test mental ages, as follows:

Tests	r	P.E.	
National Test, Scale A	.84	.01	
National Test, Scale B	.86	.01	
Haggerty Test, Delta 2	.84	.01	
Otis Advanced Examination	.80	.02	
Otis Primary Examination	.80	.02	(wide range of grades)
Mentimeter (Trabue)	.88	.09	
Dearborn, Series I	.79	.02	
Dearborn, Series II	.87	.01	
Illinois I	.74	.03	
Terman Group	.75	.02	

Stenquist (1921) worked the correlations between various intelligence tests and a composite made of many and varied tests. He finds these four tests to rank highest. The correlations found for them are as follows:

Tests	r	P.E.
National Test, Scale A	.80	.01
National Test, Scale B	.79	.01
Haggerty Test, Delta 2	.81	.01
Otis Advanced Examination	.68	.02

Elsewhere [1] he says that these four are the most widely used general intelligence tests in the grades for which they were devised.

[1] Stenquist, J. L., *Manual for Stenquist Tests of Mechanical Aptitude*, p. 3. He mentions along with these tests only two others, and both of those are for high schools.

Dr. Arthur S. Otis, of the World Book Company, has given the writer

A third reason for selecting these particular tests was that they contained a wide variety of popular sub-tests. Of the total twenty-six sub-tests used in Grades 5 to 7, twenty were sufficiently dissimilar to deserve classification into separate types. This classification is arbitrary. The division into types was based, first,

TABLE II

THE TWENTY DIFFERENT SUB-TESTS STUDIED IN GRADES 5-7 AND THE EXAMINATIONS IN WHICH EACH OCCURS

Names of Sub-Tests	Names of Tests			
	Nat. A	Nat. B	Hag. Δ2	Otis Adv.
Arithmetic Problems	I	..	I	I
Sentence Completion	I	..	..	..
Logical Selection	I	..	..	..
Synonym—Antonym (same—opposite)	I	..	I	..
Symbol Digit	I	..	..	..
Written Directions	..	..	..	I
Selection of Opposites (opposites).............	..	..	..	I
Disarranged Sentences	..	..	..	I
Matching Proverbs (proverbs).................	..	..	..	I
Geometric Figures	..	..	..	I
Analogies	..	I	..	I
Similarities	..	..	..	I
Narrative Completion	..	..	..	I
Memory	..	..	..	I
Vocabulary (sentence reading).................	..	I	I	..
Picture Completion	..	..	I	..
Best Reasons (practical judgment).............	..	..	I	..
Information	..	I	I	..
Fundamentals Arithmetic (computation).......	..	I	..	..
Visual Comparison (comparison).............	..	I	..	..

Note: The table is read as follows: 'Arithmetic Problems' was one sub-test in each of the three different tests, i.e., in **Nat. A, Hag. Δ2, and Otis Adv.**; 'Sentence Completion' was one sub-test in one of the tests, i.e., **Nat. A**; etc.

on the names given to the sub-tests by the author or authors, and second, on a common-sense study of the nature of the situations presented and responses called for. Since the facts will be presented for each sub-test separately, no importance is attached to this more or less satisfactory division, except its value in proving that the four tests contain a rather wide range of sub-tests. Not only do these examinations contain a wide range of com-

some interesting estimates in connection with the extent to which these tests have been used. He says: "I estimate that about two million children have been tested by the Otis Advanced Examination, and probably one million by the Otis Primary. I feel certain that over a million copies of each of the other tests have been used, and probably over two million of the National Intelligence Test, Scale A."

ponent tests, but they contain those which, for the most part, have
been widely used in other group tests. Take, for example, four
or five other verbal group tests suitable for use above the third
grade, and see what proportion of their sub-tests is similar in form
to those studied here. Seven out of eight sub-tests of Army Alpha
appear to be similar in form; four out of the ten in Dearborn,
Series II, Tests 4 and 5; five out of the seven in Illinois I; two
out of three of Miller (the other one being a combination of two
which are in our battery) ; seven out of ten of the Terman Group
Test. Tables II and III give a list of the tests studied.

TABLE III

THE SEVENTEEN DIFFERENT SUB-TESTS STUDIED IN GRADES 3-4 AND THE
TEST IN WHICH EACH OCCURS

Names of Sub-Tests	Names of Tests			
	Nat. A	Nat. B	Hag. Δ_2	Otis Prim.
Arithmetic Problems	I	..	I	..
Sentence Completion	I	..	..	..
Logical Selection	I	..	..	..
Synonym—Antonym (same—opposite)	I	..	I	I *
Symbol Digit	I	..	..	..
Oral Directions	..	..	..	I
Association	..	..	..	I
Maze	..	..	..	I
Picture Sequence	..	..	..	I
Similarities	..	..	..	I
Vocabulary (sentence reading)	..	I	I	..
Picture Completion	..	..	I	I
Best Reasons (practical judgment)..........	..	..	I	I *
Information	..	I	I	..
Fundamentals Arithmetic (computation).......	..	I	..	..
Analogies	..	I	..	..
Visual Comparison (comparison)............	..	I	..	..

* The administering of these two sub-tests requires so much more oral
language than the giving of those with which they are grouped that they
probably should be placed under separate headings. However, we wish
to be conservative in our statement of the number of different sub-tests,
since we do not claim these divisions to be anything but arbitrary.

Median.—There are several methods which might have been
employed in getting a composite of the results from the four
mental tests, each with some advantages and some disadvantages.
The median of the four mental ages was finally decided upon as
being as satisfactory a method as any. Any form of mean, plain
or weighted, would have given undue emphasis to extreme scores.
This appeared to be a distinct disadvantage because we had no

reason whatever to wish the extreme scores to affect especially
the composite. The median has advantage over any other measure
of central tendency, except the mode, from this one point of view.
Yule (1922, p. 120) discourages the use of the median in cases
of discontinuous variation and in cases where the series of measures is small. In general his chief objection to the use of the
median is not that it is necessarily further from the real point
of central tendency than some other measure that might be employed, but that it is more difficult to interpret mathematically.
He says that in some cases the median may be a better measure
of central tendency than the average. To quote him: "If obser-
vations of any kind are liable to present occasional greatly out-
lying values (whether real, or due to errors or blunders), the
median will be more stable and less affected by fluctuations of
sampling than the arithmetic mean." Pintner (1923, p. 78)
defends the method of using a median of mental ages as the best
guess as to the actual mental age of an individual, but it should
be said that in his illustrations of the method he does not deal
with as few as four measures. In the present study the median
was decided upon because the primary object was to obtain from
the four mental ages the most likely mental age of the child,
regardless of whether the composite mental age was subject to
algebraic treatment or not. The reason for using mental age
rather than crude score, or any other measure, is obvious: it was
the simplest and most feasible method in this case for obtaining
comparable units.

Interval Between First and Last Tests.—If the mental ages for
all tests were to be considered comparable, ideal conditions would
have demanded that all tests be given within a short space of time
—probably an interval of two or three days at the most. But
487 children with ideas of their own, together with their parents
or guardians with their ideas, and their teachers, principals, and
superintendents with their ideas, do not yield so readily to conditions which an experimenter considers ideal for his experiment,
not to mention a host of physical conditions which cannot be con-
trolled. In the Richmond sampling the longest interval between
the administering of the first and the fourth test was thirteen
days. The maximum intervals between the first and the last test
for the other samplings were as follows: For Children's University School, six days; for Monessen, one month; for Public

School No. 1, Bronx, five months; for Scarboro, eight months. It was deemed unnecessary to attempt to correct the mental ages of any of the tests for the effect of maturing in any except the last two schools.

The method of correcting for the mental growth during the testing period so as to make different mental ages comparable can best be explained by an actual illustration. The seventh grade class in Scarboro School took National A and National B on November 4, Haggerty on May 26, and Otis on May 27. February 16 would be the mid-point. We computed the I.Q. for National A, and by means of it predicted what would have been the most probable M.A. on February 16. We did the same for National B. For Haggerty and Otis the same procedure was followed, except to calculate back to February 16. The median of the theoretical mental ages was found. The C.A., of course, was also taken as of February 16. This procedure assumes the constancy of I.Q., but few of even the most critical will object to this assumption when the interval for which we are making it is never over four months. There is another criticism of more serious import. When we increased the mental age for National A from what it was on November 4 to what it would most probably be on February 16, we added on an amount to mental age which was never accounted for in terms of scores on the sub-tests.

Likewise a certain amount was deducted from the tests given in May, but nothing was ever deducted from the scores on the sub-tests. The consequence of this is that the scores for the sub-tests of examinations given later than the average tend to be too high; the scores on sub-tests for examinations given earlier than the average tend to be too low. The effect of this on the correlations between scores on the sub-tests and mental ages, and between scores on sub-tests and chronological ages, is to force them toward zero. The error involved here, however, is probably more serious theoretically than practically. In the first place, the intervals mentioned above are maximum intervals; the time span between the first and last test for every child of these schools was not as great as these figures show. Secondly, the number of cases affected by this error was not especially large. The number of children from Scarboro School, where the interval was greatest, was only twenty-seven for grades five to seven, and fourteen for grades three and four; the number from Public

School No. 1, Bronx, where the interval was next greatest (five months) was seventy-nine for grades five to seven.

Sub-Test Scores.—The scores employed for the component tests were the crude scores as weighted by the author or authors of the respective examinations. For example, in order to get the total crude score on National A, the authors direct us to multiply sub-test #1 by 2, sub-test #2 by 2, and sub-test #5 by $\frac{3}{10}$, and the others by 1. It is these scores, as weighted in the total crude score of the test, that have been used in this study.

SAMPLING

From the very outset it was clear to the writer that the results obtained in this study would be largely influenced by the nature of the sampling of the population upon which the results were based. In facing this difficulty one course of procedure, which was rather inviting, was to be fairly careful about the method of selection of cases, and then ease one's conscience at the end—if it were not at ease—by statistical refinements of the results. After considerable thought this method did not appear to be a promising one in this case. Instead of taking a sampling, working out the results, and then expressing the reliability in terms of a formula, which would demand that we assume more than we could justly assume,[1] it appeared to be a better policy to take two or three samplings, and work out all results separately. A comparison of the results based on the different samplings would act as a sort of common-sense test of reliability, in addition to any reliability figures that might be worked out by more refined methods.

Richmond Sampling.—One set of data was the test results for 208 white children of the lower half of the fifth grade of the

---

[1] There are two different lines of thought in connection with this. First, we mean that for practical purposes we do not care so much about the relations existing between a sub-test and M.A., or between a sub-test and C.A., for a perfect sampling of all the children in the United States, as we do about the relations existing in a specific school, the enrollment of which may differ considerably from the perfect sampling. An examination may yield mental ages which are considered highly accurate for a perfect sampling, but the real injustice comes when a given child is erroneously ranked in a particular school of a specific type of population. Second, one of the hypotheses with which we started was that probably better environment acted somewhat like length of life (C.A.) on mental ages. To assume a perfect sampling would be to level any effects that might come from this aspect of C.A.

public schools of Richmond, Va. Richmond is a city of 180,000 people. Though there are several private and parochial schools in the city, the majority of its children attend the public schools. The total school enrollment is 86 per cent of the total number eligible for school attendance as shown by the school census. The 208 pupils represent all the 5A[1] pupils from three different schools and seven different rooms. These particular cases were selected with no other purpose in view than that they should be typical of the city. One school was in the northern part of the city, a second in the west end, and the third was on the south side. One was in a community where, as a whole, the social status was

TABLE IV

Per Cent of Population in Various Gainful Occupations (General Divisions) for United States * and for Fathers of 208 Richmond Children

	All Male Inhabitants of U. S. 10 Yrs. Old and Over	Fathers of Richmond Children
Agriculture, Forestry, and Animal Husbandry..	.298	.015
Extractions of Minerals......................	.033	.000
Manufacturing and Mechanical Industries.......	.329	.313
Transportation	.086	.149
Trade	.108	.333
Public Service (not elsewhere classified).......	.023	.030
Professional Service	.034	.045
Domestic and Personal Service................	.037	.010
Clerical Occupations	.051	.105

* General divisions and figures for all inhabitants in gainful occupations in the United States taken from *Fourteenth Census of the United States, 1920*—Population: Occupations, p. 2, Table 2.

below the average of the city. The occupations of the parents were, in general, unskilled, semi-skilled, or skilled. Another community was one that might be considered the general average of the city. Many proprietors of small stores, office assistants, and some professional people lived in this neighborhood. The third section was above the average of the city. It was made up of proprietors of large stores, heads of real estate companies, bankers, professional people, and the like. The number of pupils from the community which was described first was 81; from the second 61; from the third 66.

The occupations of the fathers of all the pupils of the Richmond

[1] In Richmond 5A means the lower half of the 5th grade.

sampling were divided into nine groups, and compared with the figures for the United States. Although the general divisions of occupations used by the United States Bureau of Census are not arranged so as to be especially serviceable for indicating social status, a comparison between the Richmond sampling and the population of the United States as a whole, on the basis of the per cent of the total in each occupational division, will enable the reader to draw his own conclusions concerning the sampling.

It is believed that the conditions of testing were such as to make for reliable results. The children were all American born, and lived in homes where English was spoken by both parents. Not over a half dozen heard any other language at home than English. Very few of the children had ever taken a group intelligence test before this work began. In addition to these conditions, the same examiner gave all the tests and carefully supervised the scoring. The pupils were tested in their own classrooms and all distractions were reduced almost to a minimum.

Miscellaneous Sampling, Grades 5-7.—In several respects the Miscellaneous sampling stands in marked contrast to the Richmond sampling. In the first place, the children were not all from the same city. The word "Miscellaneous" is chosen for convenience to show this. Of the total 179 cases, 52 were from Monessen Public Schools, Monessen, Pa.; 21 were from the Children's University School, a rather exclusive private school, New York City; 79 were from Public School No. 1, Bronx, New York City; and 27 were from Scarboro School, an exclusive private school, Scarboro-on-Hudson, N. Y. Second, instead of having a group in the same half-grade, according to their school classification, we shall deal with pupils who were scattered over six half-grades. Again, though the pupils selected from each school are typical, we think, of the school from which they were taken, the enrollment of each school or school system was not a fair sampling of the total population of American school children. Fourth, though the experimenter took precaution not to include the test results for any child who was not American born, there is a wide range in the pupils' capacities in understanding English. The language handicap was greatest for the pupils of Public School No. 1, Bronx, where over 90 per cent of the children were of Italian parentage. The language factor was an important consideration in Monessen schools also. The United States Census of 1920 showed the total population of Monessen, all classes, to be 18,179, and of this number 11,234, or 62 per cent, were listed as native whites. With the aid of the principal of the junior high school, who knew most of the children and was familiar with all the family names, all the pupils in this study were divided into groups on the basis of nationality. By this method we found 63 per cent of our group to be from American homes. The rest of the pupils were, in about equal numbers, Italians, Slavs, and Finns. The pupils in Children's University School and in Scarboro, with two or three exceptions, came from homes where superior English was spoken.

Fifth, all the children were not equally familiar with standardized tests. It is impossible to state the differences definitely, but in general it may be said that little or no testing with group intelligence tests had been done in Monessen or in Children's University School previous to the giving of the battery here studied; much work of this nature had been done previously in Public School No. 1, Bronx, and at Scarboro. It is not believed, however, that any of the pupils who are included in this study had taken any other tests at so short an interval before this battery—if they had taken any group intelligence test at all—as to render their results incomparable to those of other pupils. Another factor that might tend slightly toward making the results of the Miscellaneous sampling different from those of Richmond is the fact that all the tests were not administered by the same examiner in the former case, nor scored by the same individuals. This might be a serious criticism, if the different examiners were not thoroughly trained. As a matter of fact, all these examinations were given by well trained examiners who used great care. The scoring was carefully done.

Lastly, a few comments of a summary nature should be made on the differences in environmental conditions existing among these 179 children. It will be remembered that in the Richmond sampling few, if any, pupils from either the very inferior or the very superior homes were included. On the contrary, the range in the Miscellaneous sampling is very wide. From homes closely bordering on tenements, where no English was heard, nor any books in English were present, except the children's school books, and where travel was impossible; to homes of the very wealthy and of the cultured, where books were supplied and reading encouraged by the parents, where the conversation was elevating, and where travel was frequent—this is the range. Many children were at or near these extremes, and our guess is that the distribution of these 179 cases, on the basis of standard of living or of environmental condition, does not approach as closely a normal curve as it does a rectangle.

Miscellaneous Sampling, Grades 3-4.—All that has been said about the Miscellaneous sampling (179 cases) in Grades 5-7 applies in a general way to a third sampling of 100 cases in Grades 3-4 from Children's University School, Monessen, and Scarboro, with the exceptions which naturally go with the fact that no pupils were included from Public School No. 1, Bronx. In order to distinguish between these two Miscellaneous samplings, we shall often refer to the pupils in Grades 5-7 as Miscellaneous sampling α, and to the pupils in Grades 3-4 as Miscellaneous sampling β.

Variability of Mental and Chronological Ages.—Before leaving the subject of sampling, a statement should be made about the ranges of mental and chronological ages. Of course, no child was included whose median mental age was dependent upon a theoretical value obtained by any extension of tables for converting crude

TABLE V

AVERAGE AND THE VARIABILITY OF MENTAL AND CHRONOLOGICAL AGES FOR EACH OF THE THREE SAMPLINGS

Sampling	Grades		Range	σ	Arith. Ave.	No. Cases
Miscellaneous α ..	5–7	M.A.	96–168	15.48	144.02	179
		C.A.	99–168	15.72	144.21	179
Richmond	5A	M.A.	96–168	12.40	132.88	208
		C.A.	101–168	13.08	134.23	208
Miscellaneous β ..	3–4	M.A.	103–153	11.86	122.26	100
		C.A.	84–178	17.74	114.60	100

scores to mental ages. In order to avoid as far as possible many of the controversial points connected with the limit of growth, no pupil was included in the Richmond sampling or the Miscellaneous sampling α (Grades 5-7) whose mental or chronological age exceeded fourteen years. This rule was followed at the expense of discarding a large number [1] of cases in the Miscellaneous sampling α. In Miscellaneous sampling β (Grades 3-4) the three

[1] If, for example, the range has been 96-198 for M.A. and 99-201 for C.A., there would have been 245 cases instead of 179. A few correlations

children whose chronological ages were between one and ten months above fourteen years were included.

The general problem to be attacked was presented in Chapter I, but a review of the central points will not be out of place here. Let us take two children whose true mental ages are equal, say eight years, but whose chronological ages differ. Let child A be seven years old, and child B ten years old. When these two children are examined on mental tests, it is conceivable that the fact that B has been experiencing situations for three years longer than A may enable him to do better on certain types of sub-tests. It is hardly possible that such an effect could be offset by any disadvantages of being in the world.[1] Any sub-test that depended upon growth in C.A. as well as in M.A. would be favoring the older child; and to the extent that it measured factors dependent upon C.A. it would be tending to give a larger M.A. to the older child. It would seem that what we desire in the M.A. technique is that mental ages should be comparable, regardless of the chronological ages that go with them. This would require that sub-tests measure mental age alone and not be dependent upon C.A.

Suppose we had a group of children who were alike in C.A. It would then be clear that for this one group of children the higher a sub-test correlated with a true measure of mental age the better the sub-test. Suppose, on the other hand, we had a group of children alike in true mental age. Then if a sub-test of some fallible examination correlated positively with C.A., that sub-test would be tending to give a higher M.A. to the older child. If we should obtain a negative correlation between a component test and C.A., we should have to assume that it was testing something which decreased as age increased. It is difficult to say just what this "something"[1] could be, but if it did exist, a sub-test would be

were worked out on the basis of these 245 cases for purposes of comparison, but nothing of significance was discovered.

[1] It is conceivable that with increase in C.A. there may go a change in interest somewhat irrespective of increase in M.A., so that some test might appeal more strongly to the younger of two children of the same M.A. Also, undesirable character traits in the field of effort, acquired the more strongly by being considered a "dummy" for a longer period, may possibly work against the older child. But this study can offer no evidence on this.

favoring the younger child to the extent to which it depended upon it. Here again we would have a sub-test that was contributing toward inequality of mental ages for pupils who have been assumed equal in mental maturity. Consequently, it would seem clear that we wish this relationship to be zero.

If we could, in practice, get the ideal conditions that we assume above, the problem would be easy,—or rather we should say it would be foolish, because if we had a measure of true mental age, we would not need to bother about these other matters. Since it is impractical to get a group of children of the same age, let us do the next best thing, viz., use the partial correlation method to render C.A. constant. And, since we do not have a true measure of mental age, let us use one of the best and most widely used measures that we have. With these changes, let us put the argument of the previous paragraphs into mathematical form. We wish:

(A) $r_{S-MA.CA}$ to be as near $+ 1.00$ as possible.

(B) $r_{S-CA.MA}$ to be as near 0 as possible.

Where S equals score on a sub-test,

Where MA equals median mental age as determined by four tests, and

Where CA equals chronological age.

For the sake of brevity, $r_{S-MA.CA}$ will be referred to often as A, and $r_{S-CA.MA}$ will be referred to as B.

We need both formula A and formula B. They do not represent two ways of saying the same thing, as may seem to be the case at first glance. It is granted that the results on formula A set limits within which the results on formula B may vary, and vice versa (for example, both could not be $+ .90$). But most of the correlations for A range between $+.3$ and $+.7$ and those for B between $- .15$ and $+ .30$, and you cannot predict results for one formula from knowledge of the results on the other. A sub-test might correlate fairly high with M.A., when C.A. is constant, and so far it is well. But it may show also considerable correlation with C.A., when the latter is allowed to vary and the M.A. is held constant. This can be illustrated by actual figures. Using the Richmond data, we find that the 'picture completion' sub-test of Haggerty Delta 2 shows a correlation of $+ .446$ with M.A.—

C.A. constant—and that the $r_{S-MA \cdot CA}$ for 'arithmetic problems' of National A is $+ .425$. Interpreting this, one might conclude that the former sub-test was measuring more of mental age than the latter. However, when we allow C.A. to vary, we find that 'picture completion' is not so desirable as it seemed at first, because it also correlates to a considerable extent with C.A. The $r_{S-CA.MA}$ is $+ .235$ for 'picture completion' and $+ .014$ for 'arithmetic problems'. This is an instance where the two methods do not rank sub-tests in the same order of preference.

The illustration just given emphasizes the fact that when results for formula A are known you may not be able to predict the order of preference that will be given to component tests by formula B, much less the actual results for B. Obviously, the same illustration, by being turned backwards, can be used to demonstrate the fact that when B ranks tests one way, you do not know how A will rank them. The logic of this is easy to see. A sub-test may show no correlation with C.A.–M.A. constant— but certainly this does not show that its $r_{S-MA.CA}$ will be high, because it is perfectly possible for a sub-test to measure neither C.A. nor M.A. The number of freckles that children of grades five to seven can count on their left hands in thirty seconds may be an example; a low score may be due to one's inability to count rapidly, but it also may be due to the fact that there are no freckles there. In such a test it is likely that $r_{S-CA.MA}$ would be low (if the results were based mainly on the scores of the girls present it *might* be negative!), but this would not give us reason to guess that $r_{S-MA.CA}$ would be high.

Since these two formulas will not rank sub-tests in the same order of excellence, we need some method of combining the two into a single measure. We know logically how we wish them to be combined. It is perfectly plain, however, that the results on A and B cannot be combined directly because of inequality of units. For example, the number of units of correspondence required to raise an r from $+ .70$ to $+ .80$ is a great deal larger than the number required to increase an r from $+ .10$ to $+ .20$.

The K-Method.—The method employed for combining the two criteria into one might be called the K-method, or the coefficient of alienation method. It simply consists in the converting of r's into K's so that they may be directly compared mathematically. The steps in the process are: (1) compute K_A, the coefficient of alienation for A; (2) compute K_B, the coefficient of alienation for B; (3) combine the results of the two in accordance with the logical principles thus far discussed. The coefficients of alienation are determined as follows:

$$K_A = \sqrt{1 - A^2}$$
$$K_B = \sqrt{1 - B^2}$$

[1]

In a sense, the coefficient of alienation is just the opposite of the coefficient of correlation, that is, the higher the coefficient of correlation the lower numerically the coefficient of alienation. Therefore, since we have set up as one part of our criterion that *the nearer A is to + 1.00 the better the sub-test,* we may say that the nearer the K_A is to + 1.00 the poorer the sub-test. The second part of our twofold criterion was that *the nearer the result of B is to 0 the better the sub-tests;* therefore, when we translate this into K we say that the higher the K_B the better the sub-test, or, what amounts to the same thing, the higher the results of $1 - K_B$ [2] the worse the sub-test. Combining these two formulas, we get $K_A + (1 - K_B)$. The higher the result on any component test in this formula the poorer the test; the lower the result the better the test. It is, therefore, an index, and for convenience in this study we shall call it the K-index. So much for the plain statement of the method, and except for a minor correction that will be discussed in the next paragraph, this is the device used for ranking the sub-tests in the three samplings.

Correction.—Even though we consider the obtained mental age as the true mental age, there is one correction that is necessary and that can be made with fair approximation. Each sub-test is being correlated against a mental age which it helped to determine. This is a situation closely similar to that which we would face if we should correlate the throw of one dice with the total throw of x dice which includes the one already thrown. Since there were four tests contributing equally [3] toward the composite M.A., and since there were five sub-tests in two of the tests (National A and

[1] See Kelley, T. L. (1923), *Statistical Method*, p. 173.
[2] I find, after having been working with this independently for some time, that Dr. E. M. Bailor (1924) has made use of this same formula in another connection, and has named it the "predictive index."
[3] This is not strictly true, because a median has been used.

National B), six in one (Haggerty Δ 2), and ten in another (Otis Adv.)—the variability in the scores on all sub-tests in a given test being about equal—each sub-test may be considered as contributing roughly $\frac{1}{20}$ (for National A and National B), $\frac{1}{24}$ (for Haggerty Δ 2), or $\frac{1}{40}$ (for Otis Adv.) toward the median mental age. Therefore r_{S-MA} and $r_{S-MA.CA}$ are too high.[1] A correction has been made for this. The method may be illustrated by taking any sub-test of National A. Suppose each score on each sub-test of National A to have a mental age equivalent. Instead of adding all mental age equivalents and dividing by 20 to get the composite M.A., let each mental age equivalent be divided by 20, and the composite will be obtained by plain summation. Now we are ready to use the formula which Thomson (1921) uses in connection with dice throws. The formula is:

$$r_{xy} = \frac{\text{Number of dice common to } x \text{ and } y \text{ throws}}{\text{Geometric mean of total dice in } x \text{ and } y \text{ throws}}$$

It will be noticed that the formula does not call for the *total of the throws,* but only for the *total number of dice in the throws.* Therefore in our analogous case it makes no difference how many sides we have to our "dice," because if the number of throws is large the mental age equivalents will be the same in both numerator and denominator and will cancel out, leaving only the number of sub-test, or "dice," in the throw. The number of "dice" in each throw, therefore, is the important matter. In National A, we have twenty "dice" in our hand. We throw one, record the total of the throw, and let it lie. This is the x throw. Next we throw the remaining nineteen, and record the total for all "dice" on the table, i.e., for the nineteen and the one. This is the y throw. Thus the correlation between any sub-test S of National A or National B, due solely to the fact that S forms a part of M.A., is as follows:

$$r_{S-MA} = \frac{1}{\sqrt{1 \times 20}} = +.224 \quad \text{for each sub-test of National A and B.}$$

$$r_{S-MA} = \frac{1}{\sqrt{1 \times 24}} = +.204 \quad \text{for each sub-test of Haggerty Delta A.}$$

[1] The correction for these two would be slightly different theoretically and our correction applies strictly to the former; but, practically, the error involved in applying it to the second would be negligible here.

$$r_{s-MA} = \frac{1}{\sqrt{1 \times 40}} = +.158 \quad \text{for each sub-test of Otis Advanced.}$$

$$r_{s-MA} = \frac{1}{\sqrt{1 \times 32}} = +.177 \quad \text{for each sub-test of Otis Primary.}$$

Compare this discussion with what is said in the Appendix I, page 70, about a similar case.

It is obvious that B is also in need of a slight correction due to the same fact that we have been discussing above, namely, that each sub-test has had a part in forming the M.A. against which it is correlated. The reason B is not exactly correct, of course, is that since r_{s-MA} is too high, the results obtained for $r_{s-CA.MA}$ will be slightly inaccurate because of the error in the restricting influence exerted by M. A. However, the error involved in allowing B to go uncorrected is so small that it will not change any figure in the first or second decimal place of the K-index. The composite ranking of the sub-test would not be changed appreciably. Consequently, no effort has been made to work out a correction for B.

Let the correction for A_m be made in the formula for the K-index.

A_m will be used to designate A as measured.

A will be reserved for A_m after it is corrected.

B_m will be used for B as measured. But since B_m goes uncorrected,

B will be used for B_m except where contrast between their meanings is needed.

r_c will be used for the correction, i.e. r between s and MA due to the fact that s is a part of MA.

K_A will be used to designate coefficient of alienation for A.

K_B will be used to designate coefficient of alienation for B.

K_c will be used to designate the K corresponding to r_c, i.e.,

$$K_c = \sqrt{1 - r_c^2}.$$

For example, the K_c for sub-tests of National A and National B is $\sqrt{1 - (.224)^2}$ or .975.

Applying the correction to A_m in the formula for the K-index, (see p. 22) we obtain the following:

$$K\text{-index} = [K_{A_m} + (1 - K_c)] + (1 - K_{B_m}), \text{ or}$$
$$K\text{-index} = K_{A_m} + 2 - (K_{B_m} + K_c).$$

But since K_c is known for all cases, we may substitute its value, and the formula becomes:

K-index $= K_{A_m} + 2 - (K_{B_m} + .975)$ for each sub-test of National A and National B.

K-index $= K_{1_m} + 2 - (K_{n_i} + .979)$ for each sub-test of Haggerty Delta 2.

K-index $= K_{A_m} + 2 - (K_{B_m} + .987)$ for each sub-test of Otis Advanced.

K-index $= K_{A_m} + 2 - (K_{B_m} + .984)$ for each sub-test of Otis Primary.

Ranks.—The K-indices having been found for all three sets of data, it only remains to rank the sub-tests in order of preference. Since we know that the higher the K-index the poorer the sub-test, we select the component test with the lowest K-index and number it 1 (i.e., the best sub-test), next lowest 2, and so on.

As is to be expected, the ranks obtained for the three samplings will not agree perfectly, but in view of the differences in the nature of the samplings, it will appear from the results which will be given in the next chapter that the agreement, with a few exceptions, is rather remarkable for the two which are strictly comparable. It will be recalled that the battery for 100 cases in Grades 3-4 was different from the batteries used with the other samplings, and that there were only twenty-four sub-tests instead of twenty-six. It is evident, therefore, that the rankings for this sampling based on the lower grades are not strictly comparable, rank for rank, with those of the other samplings. Moreover, the rank of 24 for the sampling of 100 cases is indicative of the sub-test which is poorest in a battery composed of these tests: National A, National B, Haggerty Delta 2, Otis Primary; while the rank 26 shows the poorest in a battery composed of National A, National B, Haggerty Delta 2, and Otis Advanced. The facts are given separately for each sampling, and therefore the reader can consider each set of rankings separately or make his own combination.

One Method of Combining Ranks.—This combination of the ranks is not offered as a summary of all the facts shown by the separate rankings; but it is submitted for what it may be worth to one who does not wish to make a combination of his own and is not interested in minor matters that might be debated, but who wishes to have, as far as the writer can give it in brief form, "the conclusion of the whole matter." In attempting to obtain as satisfactory a summary as possible, it was decided to use the facts from all three samplings. This forces one to assume that the mental ages obtained from the battery of tests used in Grades 3 and 4 were comparable to mental ages obtained by the other battery. This does not appear to be a violent assumption since, in our case, three-fourths of the battery is the same. Even with this assumption, of course, the ranks are not comparable, but the K-indices are. The composite rank for each sub-test of National A, National B and Haggerty Delta 2 was found as follows:

$$\frac{3(K\text{-index for Richmond}) + 2(K\text{-index for Misc. } \alpha) + 1(K\text{-index for Misc. } \beta)}{6}$$

The composite for each sub-test of Otis Advanced Examination was found as follows:

$$\frac{3(K\text{-index for Richmond}) + 2(K\text{-index for Miscellaneous } \alpha)}{5}$$

The rank for each sub-test of Otis Primary was simply the rank as obtained for the 100 children in Grades 3 and 4.

Weights that are assigned in cases like this appear to be too dependent upon the judgment of the experimenter, but the writer offers two reasons for the weights given. First, there were more children examined in the Richmond sampling than in the Miscellaneous sampling α and more in Miscellaneous α than in Miscellaneous β. Second, it was thought that the Richmond sampling was a little more typical of conditions found in practical situations over the country than either of the other two. Consider, for example, the matter of language handicaps. We think that the pupils of a given school would be more homogeneous in language capacity than those of the Miscellaneous samplings. Moreover, as a practical matter in making school adjustments to individual differences, errors in the relative intelligence ratings of children in about the same school grade would cause more injustice than errors in rating children with respect to others spread over several grades. Errors in relative ratings often cause more misunderstandings than errors in absolute ratings. The Richmond sampling is a group of such a nature that this problem of mis-measurement is presented in a situation more similar to the ones with which schoolmen will have to deal. Too much importance, however, should not be attached to this last thought, because, though the practical side should not be lost from sight, the results of this study will be of more interest probably from the theoretical point of view.

CHAPTER III

DETAILS OF STATISTICAL PROCEDURES, AND RESULTS

Coefficients of Correlation.—Our purpose at the beginning was to compute all coefficients of correlation by the original Pearson 'product moment' formula. However, the adaptation of the 'product moment' method used in the Otis Correlation Chart was found very convenient, and was used throughout the study. The formula upon which the Otis Chart depends is as follows:

$$r = \frac{(\Sigma X^2 + \Sigma Y^2 - \Sigma V^2) - 2\Sigma X \Sigma Y \div N}{2\sqrt{[\Sigma X^2 - (\Sigma X)^2 \div N][\Sigma Y^2 - (\Sigma Y)^2 \div N]}}$$

Where Σ = sum.
" $V = Y - X$.
" X, Y, and V = measures from arbitrary zero points.
" N = number of cases.

A comparison between the results obtained by this and the 'product moment' methods is expressed by Otis as follows: "The coefficient by this chart is exactly the same to any number of decimal places as if calculated by the regular (Pearson) 'product moment' formula:

$$r = \frac{\Sigma xy}{\sqrt{\Sigma x^2 \ \Sigma y^2}}$$

when true means are used and may be said therefore to have been calculated by the 'product-moment method' to distinguish it from one calculated by any of the approximate methods such as the 'foot rule' or rank methods."[1]

The reliability of each r was computed by the regular formula:

P.E.$_r$ = .6745σ_r, or .6745$\dfrac{1 - r^2}{\sqrt{N}}$. Table VI gives the coefficient

of correlation between each sub-test and M.A., between M.A. and

[1] Otis, Arthur S., *Directions: Otis Correlation Chart,* World Book Company. See also *Statistical Method in Educational Measurement,* pp. 189 ff. by the same author. Also *Journal of Educational Research,* Vol. 8, pp. 440-448.

C.A., and between each sub-test and C.A., for the three samplings separately, and the measure of reliability for each coefficient.

In applying the 'product moment' method to the data, we have, of course, assumed rectilinearity in regression. This assumption has not been justified in every case. In a few places where it appeared that a line through the actual means of the arrays would depart considerably from a straight line, the correlation ratio was computed. These results will be reported in Chapter IV. Though something would probably have been added by computing the correlation ratios for all sub-tests in each sampling, the result would not have justified the enormous amount of labor required. As will be shown in a later chapter, it does not appear that errors great enough to invalidate general conclusions have resulted from making this assumption of rectilinearity of regression.

In order to assist the reader to envisage the figures of Table VI a series of small tables will be given. It is needless to say that these minor tables are presenting not more but less than the original one, but they may prove to be of some value in directing the reader's attention to general trends in so far as this table enables one to discover them. Of the twenty-six r's given in the M.A. column for the Richmond data in Table VI, roughly one-fourth fall between $+ .67$ and $+ .72$. (See Table VII (a).) The mid-score of this highest quarter-group proved to be $+ .69$. The sub-tests which fall in this highest quarter are as follows: sub-tests #2 and #3 of National A; sub-test #7 of Otis Advanced; #6 of Haggerty Delta 2; and #2 and #4 of National B. Other parts of Table VII are read in the same way. For example, in sub-division (f) it will be seen that one-fourth of the sub-tests correlate with C.A. to the extent of $- .35$ to $- .16$ in Miscellaneous sampling β, and that these sub-tests are as follows: #2, #4, and #5 of National A; #7 of Otis Primary; #1 and #4 of Haggerty Delta 2.

The facts presented in Tables VI, VIII and IX form the heart of this study. In the discussions to be offered in the following chapters frequent reference will be made to the results presented in these three tables. Since this is true, and since the tables are self-explanatory, it is unnecessary to comment on them in this chapter, except to direct the reader's special attention to two or three points in connection with each. In Table VI it should be noted that: (1) All values for the M.A. columns are positive, showing that all

TABLE VI

COEFFICIENTS OF CORRELATION, TOGETHER WITH THEIR RELIABILITIES, BETWEEN SUB-TESTS AND MENTAL AGES AND BETWEEN SUB-TESTS AND CHRONOLOGICAL AGES FOR THREE SAMPLINGS

Test and Sub-Tests	Richmond 5A Grade (208 cases)				Misc. α Grades 5-7 (179 cases)				Misc. β Grades 3-4 (100 cases)			
	M.A.	P.E.	C.A.	P.E.	M.A.	P.E.	C.A.	P.E.	M.A.	P.E.	C.A.	P.E.
NATIONAL A												
1. Arithmetic Problems	+.431	.038	−.079	.047	+.315	.046	+.109	.049	+.623	.041	−.040	.067
2. Sentence Completion	+.677	.026	−.116	.046	+.811	.017	−.296	.046	+.685	.036	−.247	.063
3. Logical Selection	+.707	.024	−.121	.046	+.634	.030	−.340	.044	+.638	.040	+.055	.067
4. Synonym-Antonym	+.601	.030	−.114	.046	+.677	.027	−.301	.045	+.501	.051	−.252	.063
5. Symbol Digit	+.362	.040	+.092	.046	+.128	.049	+.253	.047	+.460	.053	−.348	.059
OTIS ADVANCED												
1. Written Directions	+.463	.037	−.119	.046	+.589	.033	−.348	.044				
2. Selection of Opposites	+.632	.028	−.202	.045	+.604	.032	−.229	.047				
3. Disarranged Sentences	+.576	.031	−.023	.047	+.451	.040	−.076	.050				
4. Matching Proverbs	+.497	.035	−.087	.047	+.540	.035	−.267	.046				
5. Arithmetic Problems	+.518	.034	−.139	.046	+.454	.040	+.065	.050				
6. Geometric Figures	+.485	.036	−.062	.047	+.526	.036	−.286	.046				
7. Analogies	+.674	.026	−.162	.046	+.678	.027	−.279	.046				
8. Similarities	+.595	.030	−.264	.044	+.604	.032	−.324	.045				
9. Narrative Completion	+.452	.037	−.129	.046	+.545	.035	−.089	.050				
10. Memory	+.638	.027	−.152	.046	+.642	.029	−.340	.044				
HAGGERTY DELTA 2												
1. Vocabulary or Sent. Read.	+.578	.031	−.104	.047	+.622	.031	−.277	.046	+.508	.050	−.324	.060
2. Arithmetic Problems	+.479	.036	+.056	.047	+.505	.038	−.063	.050	+.637	.040	+.031	.067
3. Picture Completion	+.407	.039	−.125	.046	+.166	.049	+.196	.048	+.347	.059	−.003	.067
4. Synonym-Antonym	+.550	.033	−.116	.046	+.588	.033	−.333	.044	+.594	.044	−.262	.063
5. Best Reasons	+.558	.032	−.157	.046	+.721	.024	−.265	.046	+.633	.040	−.083	.067
6. Information	+.719	.023	−.188	.045	+.783	.019	−.242	.047	+.727	.032	−.032	.067
NATIONAL B												
1. Fundamentals Arithmetic.	+.351	.041	−.128	.046	+.073	.050	+.280	.046	+.485	.052	+.079	.067
2. Information	+.702	.024	−.163	.046	+.726	.024	−.227	.047	+.604	.043	−.066	.067
3. Vocabulary or Sent. Read.	+.569	.032	−.007	.047	+.660	.028	−.446	.047	+.647	.039	−.086	.067
4. Analogies	+.676	.026	−.245	.044	+.666	.028	−.159	.049	+.443	.054	−.098	.067
5. Visual Comparison	+.260	.044	−.131	.046	+.034	.050	+.383	.043	+.088	.067	+.295	.062
OTIS PRIMARY												
1. Oral Directions									+.571	.045	−.040	.067
2. Associations									+.160	.066	+.120	.067
3. Picture Completion									+.251	.063	+.050	.067
4. Maze									+.485	.052	+.041	.067
5. Picture Sequence									+.439	.054	+.161	.066
6. Similarities									+.382	.057	+.000	.067
7. Synonym-Antonym									+.389	.052	−.155	.067
8. Best Reasons									+.510	.050	+.125	.066
C.A. (Chronological Age)	−.210	.045			−.280	.046			−.061	.067		

TABLE VII

GROUPING OF FIGURES PRESENTED IN TABLE VI

Ranges in *r* Containing ¼ of Sub-Tests	Midscores of Quarter Groups	Nat. A Sub-Test #	Otis * Sub-Test #	Hag. Δ2 Sub-Test #	Nat. B Sub-Test #
(a) M.A. Column, Richmond Data, Grade 5A.					
+.67 to +.72	+.69	2, 3	7	6	2, 4
+.57 to +.64	+.60	4	2, 3, 8, 10	1	3
+.46 to +.56	+.50	..	1, 4, 5, 6	2, 4, 5	..
+.26 to +.45	+.38	1, 5	9	3	1, 5
(b) M.A. Column, Miscellaneous Data α, Grades 5-7.					
+.68 to +.81	+.72	2, 4	7	5, 6	2
+.60 to +.67	+.63	3	2, 8, 10	1	3, 4
+.45 to +.59	+.54	..	1, 4, 5, 6, 9	2, 4	..
+.03 to +.45	+.15	1, 5	3	3	1, 5
(c) M.A. Column, Miscellaneous Data β, Grades 3-4.					
+.63 to +.73	+.64	2, 3	..	2, 5, 6	3
+.51 to +.62	+.58	1	1, 8	1, 4	2
+.44 to +.50	+.48	4, 5	4, 7	..	1, 4
+.09 to +.44	+.25	..	2, 3, 5, 6	3	5
(d) C.A. Column, Richmond Data, Grade 5A.					
−.06 to +.13	+.03	5	6, 3	2, 3	3
−.12 to −.08	−.11	2, 4, 1	1, 4	1, 4	..
−.16 to −.12	−.13	3	5, 9, 10	5	1, 5
−.26 to −.16	−.20	..	2, 7, 8	6	2, 4
(e) C.A. Column, Miscellaneous Data α, Grades 5-7.					
+.07 to +.38	+.23	1, 5	5	3	1, 5
−.24 to −.06	−.16	..	2, 9, 3	2, 6	2, 4
−.30 to −.25	−.28	2	4, 6, 7	1, 5	3
−.35 to −.30	−.34	3, 4	1, 8, 10	4	..
(f) C.A. Column, Miscellaneous Data β, Grades 3-4.					
+.06 to +.30	+.17	3	2, 5	..	1, 4, 5
−.03 to +.05	+.02	..	3, 4, 6	2, 3, 6	..
−.13 to −.04	−.07	1	1, 8	5	2, 3
−.35 to −.16	1.26	2, 4, 5	7	1, 4	..

* In sub-divisions that deal with Miscellaneous β, the facts refer to Otis Primary; in all other cases the reference is to Otis Advanced.

the sub-tests correlate to *some* extent with M.A., as it is here measured. (2) The range of *r*'s in the M.A. columns is wide, the highest being + .783 for sub-test #6 ('information') in Haggerty Delta 2 in the Miscellaneous sampling α, and the lowest being + .034 for sub-test #5 ('visual comparison') in National B in the same sampling. This indicates that there is a wide difference in the extent to which the various sub-tests measure mental age, even if we do not raise the question of how much the sub-tests are affected by other factors than brightness.   This fact alone would show the necessity of a study like the present one, because when a sub-test like 'visual comparison', 'symbol-digit', or 'picture completion' shows very low correlations with M.A., one begins to wonder if it is not measuring something else in addition to M.A. A low correlation with M.A. does not necessarily mean this, because it is conceivable that a sub-test could measure M.A. to a small extent and yet not measure anything irrelevant to mental maturity; but, on the other hand, when there is so much of the measuring capacity of the variable not functioning in measuring M.A.,[1] we may at least become suspicious that it may be lending itself to the measurement of factors that have nothing to do with brightness or mental maturity.   (3) The majority of the r's in the C.A. columns are negative.   It is interesting to compare these columns with the respective columns of Table VIII.

Partial Correlations.—It has already been explained in a previous chapter that we wish two partials: first, A_m, or $r_{S-MA.CA}$, and second, B_m, or $r_{S-CA.MA}$.   These were computed for all samplings by the regular method.[2]   The results are given in Table VIII.

In Table VIII the following facts should be noted: (1) As is to be expected from the facts of the preceding table, all the results for A_m are positive.   (2) About one-half of the results for B_m are positive.   (3) It will be noticed that the results on A_m and on B_m seem to be independent of one another; that is, when A_m is high, one cannot predict anything concerning the height of B_m, and vice versa; from knowledge of A_m, one does not even know whether the results for B_m will be positive, zero, or negative. (4) The different figures obtained in the various samplings may appear very confusing.   Table IX will be a great aid in sum-

---

[1] Note that the M.A. referred to here is based chiefly on tests of verbal abstract ability.

[2] Yule, G. Udny (1922), *Introduction to the Theory of Statistics*, p. 239, gives the formula for three variables as follows:

$$r_{12.} = \frac{r_{12} - r_{13} \cdot r_{23}}{\sqrt{1 - r_{13}{}^2} \; \sqrt{1 - r_{23}{}^2}}.$$

Converting this into the symbols used in this study, we get:

$$A_m, \text{ or } r_{S-MA.CA} = \frac{r_{S-MA} - r_{S-CA} \cdot r_{MA-CA}}{\sqrt{1 - r^2{}_{S-CA}} \; \sqrt{1 - r^2{}_{MA-CA}}}$$

$$\text{and } B_m, \text{ or } r_{S-CA.MA} = \frac{r_{S-CA} - r_{S-MA} \cdot r_{MA-CA}}{\sqrt{1 - r^2{}_{S-MA}} \; \sqrt{1 - r^2{}_{MA-CA}}}.$$

TABLE VIII

SHOWING THE PARTIAL CORRELATIONS A OR $r_{S-MA.CA}$ AND B OR $r_{S-CA.MA}$ FOR ALL SUB-TESTS IN THE THREE SAMPLINGS

Tests and Sub-Tests	Richmond Grade 5A 208 Cases		Misc. a Grades 5-7 179 Cases		Misc. β Grades 3-4 100 Cases	
	A_m	B_m	A_m	B_m	A_m	B_m
NATIONAL A						
1. Arithmetic Problems	+ .425	+ .014	+ .363	+ .216	+ .623	— .003
2. Sentence Completion	+ .673	+ .036	+ .794	— .123	+ .693	— .282
3. Logical Selection	+ .703	+ .039	+ .598	— .218	+ .644	+ .121
4. Synonym-Antonym	+ .594	+ .015	+ .648	— .157	+ .503	— .256
5. Symbol Digit	+ .391	+ .184	+ .214	+ .304	+ .469	— .361
OTIS ADVANCED						
1. Written Directions	+ .451	— .025	+ .546	— .236	....	....
2. Selection of Opposites.....	+ .617	— .091	+ .578	— .078	....	....
3. Disarranged Sentences	+ .586	+ .123	+ .449	+ .058	....	....
4. Matching Proverbs	+ .492	+ .020	+ .502	— .144	....	....
5. Arithmetic Problems	+ .505	— .024	+ .493	+ .225	....	....
6. Geometric Figures	+ .484	+ .047	+ .485	— .170	....	....
7. Analogies	+ .663	— .028	+ .651	— .126	....	....
8. Similarities	+ .573	— .177	+ .565	— .203	....	....
9. Narrative Completion	+ .438	— .039	+ .544	+ .080	....	....
10. Memory	+ .627	— .024	+ .606	— .217	....	....
HAGGERTY Δ2						
1. Vocabulary, or Sent. Read.	+ .572	+ .021	+ .589	— .137	+ .517	— .341
2. Arithmetic Problems	+ .503	+ .183	+ .508	+ .094	+ .640	+ .091
3. Picture Completion	+ .446	+ .235	+ .239	+ .259	+ .348	+ .019
4. Synonym-Antonym	+ .542	.000	+ .547	— .216	+ .600	— .282
5. Best Reasons	+ .544	— .049	+ .699	— .095	+ .631	— .057
6. Information	+ .708	— .054	+ .768	— .039	+ .727	+ .017
NATIONAL B						
1. Fundamentals Arithmetic..	+ .334	— .059	+ .164	+ .314	+ .492	+ .125
2. Information	+ .693	— .023	+ .708	— .036	+ .602	— .036
3. Vocabulary, or Sent. Read.	+ .581	+ .139	+ .635	— .085	+ .646	— .061
4. Analogies	+ .659	— .143	+ .655	+ .038	+ .452	+ .140
5. Visual Comparison	+ .239	— .067	+ .159	+ .409	+ .111	+ .302
OTIS PRIMARY						
1. Oral Directions	....	....	....	....	+ .571	— .006
2. Associations	....	....	....	....	+ .169	+ .132
3. Picture Completion	....	....	....	....	+ .255	+ .067
4. Maze	....	....	....	....	+ .489	+ .081
5. Picture Sequence	....	....	....	....	+ .456	+ .210
6. Similarities	....	....	....	....	+ .391	+ .026
7. Synonym-Antonym	....	....	....	....	+ .474	— .144
8. Best Reasons	....	....	....	....	+ .507	— .110

marizing the facts, but one can see definite trends in this table. For example, when A_m and B_m are considered together, some sub-tests show definite tendencies in all samplings to rank low on the basis of the criterion; 'visual comparison' is an illustration. There are others which show tendencies to rank high in all samplings; 'analogies' or 'information,' for example.

K-indices and Ranks.—Following the formula given in the previous chapter, page 24, the K-index for each sub-test was computed. On the basis of these indices the sub-tests were assigned ranks. A composite ranking was given to the sub-tests finally; but the method of arriving at this composite was somewhat arbitrary because weights were given to the indices without any mathematical justification, and too much confidence should not be placed in this one set of figures. It will be recalled that the weights assigned to the K-indices in order to get the composite indices were as follows: 3 for Richmond data, 2 for Miscellaneous sampling α, Grades 5-7, and 1 for the 3rd and 4th grade sampling. The variability was practically the same for each series of K-indices entering into the averages. This is shown by the values for Q in Table IX. The weighted averages and the accompanying ranks are given, as has been stated before, for what they may be worth to those who may desire that the writer give in one set of figures what he considers to be the most just summary of his findings. Reasons have been given elsewhere why it is felt that these weighted results represent the best single measures, but since the reasons given may not be convincing, a column giving plain averages is also included. We do not mean to imply that we have obviated the weighting difficulty by use of plain averages. It is obvious that a plain average, assuming equal variabilities for all factors, is merely a special type of weighted average, viz., one where all component parts receive a weight of 1. However, there seems to be a popular feeling that in case of the plain average there is less opportunity for manipulation of figures in the hands of the experimenter. In a thesis, which I read recently, in a professional library, the author had expended great labor to build up a system of weights for his many variables. At the end, however, a set of plain averages had been included for purposes of comparison. On the margin of the page beside the plain averages an anonymous critic had written "non-doctored."

Attention is called to the following facts in connection with

TABLE IX

SHOWING K-INDICES AND RANKS FOR THREE SAMPLINGS SEPARATELY, AND AVERAGES BASED UPON THE INDICES

SUB-TESTS	Richmond 208 Cases		Misc. α 179 Cases		Misc. β 100 Cases		Weighted Average		Plain Ave.	
	K-index	Rank	K-index	Rank	K-index	Rank	K-index	Rank	K-index	Rank
NATIONAL B										
1. Arithmetic Problems	.931	22	.981	22	.807	7	.928	22	.906	22
2. Sentence Completion	.765	5	.641	1	.787	2	.728	2	.731	2
3. Logical Selection	.737	2	.850	12	.797	5	.785	5	.795	5
4. Synonym-Antonym	.829	9	.799	7	.922	15	.835	11	.852	11
5. Symbol Digit	.962	24	1.049	24	.975	21	.993	25	.995	25
OTIS ADVANCED										
1. Written Directions	.906	19.5	.879	15			.895	20.5	.893	19.5
2. Selection of Opposites	.800	8	.832	9.5			.813	9	.816	9
3. Disarranged Sentences	.831	10	.909	20.5			.862	14	.870	15
4. Matching Proverbs	.884	17	.888	18			.886	17	.886	18
5. Arithmetic Problems	.876	16	.909	20.5			.889	18	.893	19.5
6. Geometric Figures	.889	18	.905	19			.895	20.5	.896	21
7. Analogies	.762	4	.980	5			.769	4	.771	4
8. Similarities	.849	13	.859	14			.853	12	.874	12
9. Narrative Completion	.913	21	.855	13			.890	19	.884	17
10. Memory	.792	7	.832	9.5			.868	16	.812	7
HAGGERTY DELTA 2										
1. Vocabulary or Sentence Reading	.841	11	.838	11	.937	19	.856	13	.872	16
2. Arithmetic Problems	.902	19.5	.886	17	.793	4	.879	16	.860	13
3. Picture Completion	.944	23	1.026	23	.958	20	.974	23	.976	23
4. Synonym-Antonym	.861	14.5	.882	16	.862	10	.868	15	.868	14
5. Best Reasons	.861	14.5	.741	4	.799	6	.811	8	.800	6
6. Information	.727	1	.662	2	.708	1	.702	1	.699	1
NATIONAL B										
1. Fundamentals Arithmetic	.968	25	1.062	25	.904	13	.989	24	.978	24
2. Information	.746	3	.732	3	.824	8	.754	3	.767	3
3. Vocabulary or Sentence Reading	.849	12	.802	8	.790	3	.824	10	.814	8
4. Analogies	.787	6	.782	6	.927	16	.809	7	.832	10
5. Visual Comparison	.996	26	1.099	26	1.066	24	1.042	26	1.054	26
Q (SEMI-INTERQUARTILE RANGE)	.06		.06		.07					
OTIS PRIMARY										
1. Oral Directions					.837	9				
2. Association					1.011	23				
3. Picture Completion					.985	22				
4. Maze					.891	12				
5. Picture Sequence					.928	17				
6. Similarities					.936	18				
7. Synonym-Antonym					.907	14				
8. Best Reasons					.884	11				

Table IX: (1) The table summarizes the figures so that the agreement, or lack of it, among all samplings can be readily seen. The K-indices for the various samplings are roughly comparable, and therefore the agreement can be read from them. (2) The ranks are merely common-sense devices employed to bring the outstanding facts to a focus. The reader will recall that while the ranks for Richmond (Grade 5A) and for Miscellaneous α (Grades 5-7) can be compared rank for rank, the ones for Miscellaneous β (Grades 3-4) are not quite comparable with these two, because there were twenty-six sub-tests in the battery used in the first two samplings and only twenty-four in that used in the third. Consequently a rank of 26 indicates the poorest sub-test in Richmond and Miscellaneous α, while 24 is the rank given to the poorest in Miscellaneous β. For our purposes this will cause little confusion. However, if one wishes to get the 1-24 ranks of the Grade 3-4 sampling into terms of the 1-26 ranks of the other two, he may do it roughly by multiplying each rank of the former by 1.08. (3) It will be noticed that the figures for Richmond and Miscellaneous α agree more closely with one another than either of these do with the third sampling. Our original data are insufficient for use in an exhaustive study of even the outstanding discrepancies. However, something will be said concerning them in the next chapter. (4) It will be observed that some of the K-indices are over 1.00. This would be impossible in the case of K, for the coefficient of alienation approaches 1.00 as a limit; but since the K-index represents a sum of K_A and $1 - K_B$, it is possible for the index to exceed 1.00.

When one examines Table IX more closely, his attention is apt to be attracted by the sub-tests at the extremes. That is, he will probably note, among other things, that the five sub-tests which receive the highest ranks are: 'information' (Haggerty Delta 2, #1), 'sentence completion' (National A, #2), 'information' (National B, #2), 'analogies' (Otis Advanced, #7), and 'logical selection' (National A, #3). He will also note that the lowest five ranks are assigned to the following: 'visual comparison' (National B, #5), 'symbol-digit' (National A, #5), 'fundamentals in arithmetic' (National B, #1), 'picture completion' (Haggerty Delta 2, #3), and 'arithmetic problems' (National A, #1). In connection with these facts at least two important questions may arise. First, what effect does the amount of time taken by a sub-test have upon its rank? In other words, what part has the factor of testing time had upon the ranks received by various sub-tests? Second, does the fact that the sub-test 'information' occurs twice in the total battery of tests boost its rank at the expense of some other sub-tests? Upon studying the facts bearing on the first question, it was found that the amount of testing time required by the five highest ranking sub-tests was 18 minutes, while that required by the five ranking lowest was 17 minutes. The correlation ('product-moment') between the weighted K-indices and the testing time of the sub-test was $+ .26 \pm .12$. The reader is reminded of the fact that the higher the index the poorer the sub-test; therefore this correlation means that for the samplings of the population here studied a very slight negative correlation exists between the testing time and the excellence of a sub-test, so far as the 26 [1] sub-tests studied are concerned. Obviously these figures are given solely to show that the time element was not a big factor in determining these particular ranks; they have little if any bearing on the general problem of the effect of testing time on the excellence of a sub-test.

The second question cannot be answered so easily. If the criticism is raised that the correlation between the scores on the sub-test 'information' and mental ages is spurious because this sub-test occurs twice in the composite by which the mental ages were determined, the criticism cannot be met squarely with facts. It should be pointed out, however, that 'arithmetic problems' occurs three times and 'fundamentals of arithmetic' once, and yet these sub-tests rank rather low in all samplings except Miscellaneous β. In this latter case there are other factors operating which will be discussed in Chapter IV. There is a second method of attacking the problem. Since these sub-tests are parts of examinations that have been devised and recommended by expert workers in this field as devices for measuring verbal abstract intelligence, how do we know that the 'information' sub-test is not measuring something that *should* be weighted heavily in the criterion? But now we see that the original question is superficially stated when it is confined only to sub-tests which bear the same names. Shall we consider the two 'information' sub-tests—

---

[1] The ranks assigned the sub-tests of Otis Primary Examination were based on only 100 cases, and therefore it seemed undesirable to include them in this study of the time factor.

which correlate with one another only to the extent .85—as measuring the same thing twice, merely because they are referred to by the same name, and assume that 'analogies', 'logical selection', and the like, are measuring something so different from 'information' as not to be a part of the same problem? The criticism, therefore, cannot be answered, because it is directed against the mental ages that form a part of our criterion. Since no one knows what proportion of an entire intelligence examination should be devoted to the testing of the ability to give analogies, to the testing of the ability to answer general information questions, to the measuring of the ability to complete sentences, and the like, it is impossible to give evidence for or against the criticism. The measures of mentality that enter into the criterion must be either accepted or rejected.

Conclusion.—It is evident that there are many aspects of the results presented here that must be examined at some length before any general conclusions are justifiable. Nevertheless, the main point upon which the study hinges is presenting itself with unmistakable emphasis, viz., that there are great differences among subtests in the degree to which they measure mental maturity irrespective of other things which have nothing to do with mentality. All that is to be said from this point on is for the purpose of giving more evidence on this fact and for the purpose of interpreting its meaning in the theory of mental measurement. It is hoped, of course, that the method of attack employed here may be of some value in the solution of the problem emphasized, but whether one agrees fully with this method of attack or not, we believe he will agree that the method is at least sufficient to show the seriousness of the problem in the theory of intelligence testing, especially as it is applied to the field of group tests.

CHAPTER IV

PART I

ADAPTABILITY OF SUB-TESTS TO SPECIAL RANGES OF M.A. AND C.A.

One of the points that seems fairly certain in the case of the Binet-Simon tests is that some sub-tests are applicable to only a narrow range of mental maturity, while others can be used for measurement of intelligence over a wider range. For example, 'finding of omission in pictures' is not used above the six-year level of mental age, though it seems that a series of this type of test could have been made sufficiently difficult to serve at higher levels. Presumably, this type was considered good up to a certain point in indicating mental maturity, but beyond that not so serviceable. On the other hand, the vocabulary test is applied over a wide range. But in spite of the precaution taken to use sub-tests over only the narrow ranges of mental maturity to which they had proved applicable, the Binet-Simon method has been criticized by many writers [1] because too little attention has been paid to the problem of whether or not each sub-test is suitable for use when there is a wide range in chronological age.

In group tests we do not have the narrow ranges in either mental maturity or chronological age. That is, the same types of tests are considered applicable as a measure of intelligence to children from Grades 3 to 8 in some cases, with all the spread in M.A. and C.A. that this may entail. The major part of our results thus far, for example, have been based upon children from about 98 to 168 months in C.A. and in M.A. Especially in group tests, therefore, the question as to whether a sub-test is equally good or equally poor all along the line seems worthy of some thought.

The main issue up to this point has been the ranking of sub-tests on the basis of their excellence in satisfying a certain

---

[1] Among those who have commented on this from one angle or another, or given figures concerning it, are: Bickersteth, Chapman and Dale, Claparede, Meumann, Pintner and Patterson, Stern, Taylor, Whipple and Yerkes. For references to articles, see Bibliography.

criterion, the assumption being made that if a sub-test is ranked high it is a good test for a battery. But this assumption is not valid until we have defined the range over which the battery is to be used. Suppose we define this very conservatively, and say that our ranks refer to the order of preference of sub-tests in a battery which is to be used over the same range as here studied. A practical question still remains: Does a given sub-test show any tendency to be a better measure within certain range of mental age, or within certain range of chronological age, than for the entire range? Is each component test of an examination which purports to measure intelligence over so wide a range of grades as 3 to 8 (and ages both mental and chronological, which this would demand) included because it has been shown applicable to this range; or is it used because it was desirable for practical purposes to have an examination that could be applied over so wide a range, and each sub-test which was good, in general, was simply enlisted, the only requirement being that the battery as a whole show a satisfactory amount of agreement with some criterion? A critical reader who wishes to know whether a low rank obtained by some particular sub-test was the result of the test's being comparatively poor all along the line or the result of the sub-test's being stretched over a wider range than that for which it was suited, cannot find out from any results thus far given. The partial correlation formula takes into account only the total r's as they exist. No idea is given of how accurately the r's tell the story for relationships that exist for narrower ranges than the whole, or, indeed, how accurately they report the correspondence for the whole range if there is any doubt about the assumption of linearity of regression.

As a consequence of what has just been said, any sub-test, 'arithmetic problems' for example, might show a K-index by which it would be ranked sixteenth on the basis of the whole range of M.A. and C.A. studied, but might have been ranked sixth, say, if the range had been narrowed to 110-144. 'Arithmetic problems' has been chosen for illustration because, upon examination of all the scatter diagrams, the distribution for this sub-test appeared to the writer to have a more marked tendency than any other to be non-rectilinear. The remainder of this chapter will be devoted to a detailed study of this sub-test from this point of view.

The Method.—The method of attacking this problem consists

of a comparison between the regression lines for the coefficient
of correlation and the lines through the actual means of the arrays.
The method, therefore, is more or less an inspectional or graphic
one, and the results do not lend themselves readily to mathematical
treatment. Of course we can compare each coefficient of correlation with the respective correlation ratios, and report as to whether
or not we are justified in assuming linearity of regression for the
whole distribution. This is done in Part II of this chapter. But

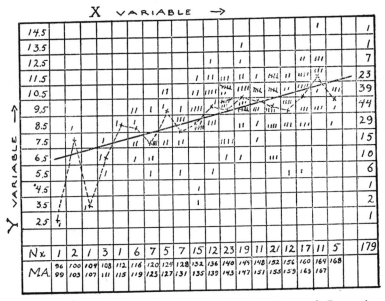

Fig. 1. *Correlation Table Showing Regression Line and Regression
Curve for y on x, or 'Arithmetic Problems' (Haggerty Delta 2, #2) on
M.A., for Miscellaneous Sampling α, Grades 5-7.*

what we want to know here is not whether, for the *whole distribution,* each correlation ratio is a given amount higher than the
coefficient of correlation, but whether, for one *part* of the distribution, the correlation technique is less applicable than for
another part. If this were found to be true, we should be led
to conclude that the sub-test is better within a certain part of the
range than it is for the whole, since we are committed at the
present time to the use of correlation in determining whether a
sub-test is good or bad.[1]

---

[1] See footnote on p. 49 for a brief discussion of this last clause.

Because of the difficulty of reproduction only one correlation table will be included as an illustration, but several diagrams showing the actual positions of the regression lines and the regression curves will be given. In correlating 'arithmetic problems' against M.A. we found the η_{yx} [1] was in every case larger than η_{xy}. Consequently in every instance we have plotted the curves (or rather the broken lines) for η_{yx} and compared them with the regression lines b_{yx}. For sake of comparison, one diagram is given

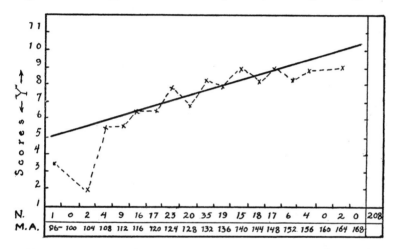

Fig. 2. *Regression Line and Regression Curve for y on x, or 'Arithmetic Problems' (Haggerty Delta 2, #2) on M.A., for Richmond Sampling.*

for η_{xy} and b_{xy}. In two diagrams, also, the lines are given for C.A. versus 'arithmetic problems'.

In all the figures, 1-9, the variable along the vertical line will be referred to as the Y-variable, and in each case it will be the crude score on a sub-test. The intervals along the horizontal line will be referred to as the X-variable, and will always represent either mental age or chronological age. A solid line will represent the regression line in each figure. A broken line will be used to connect the actual means of the arrays for one variable corresponding to given values of the other. These broken lines will be referred to as regression curves.

[1]η_{yx} is employed according to conventional usage to mean correlation ratio of y on x, where y refers to score on sub-test, and x to M.A. b_{yx} means the straight line regression of y on x.

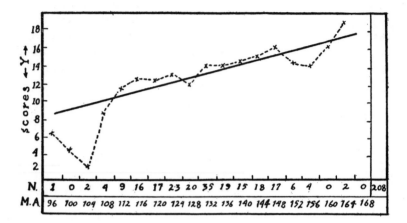

FIG. 3. *Regression Line and Regression Curve for y on x, or 'Arith-metic Problems' (National A, #1) on M.A., for Richmond Sampling.*

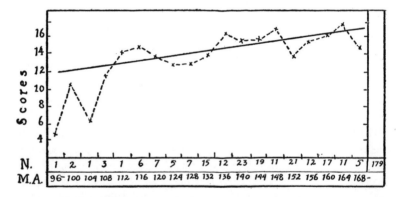

FIG. 4. *Regression Line and Regression Curve for y on x, or 'Arith-metic Problems' (National A, #1) on M.A., for Miscellaneous Sampling α, Grades 5-7.*

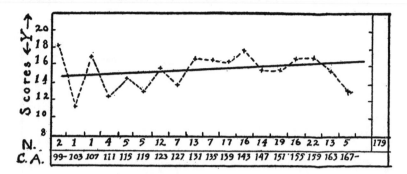

FIG. 5. *Regression Line and Regression Curve for y on x, or 'Arithmetic Problems' (National A, #1) on C.A., for Miscellaneous Sampling a, Grades 5-7.*

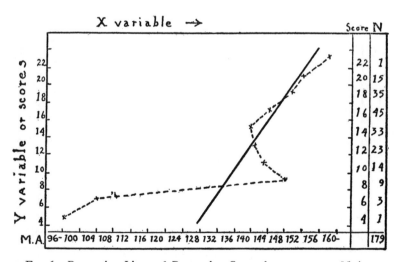

FIG. 6. *Regression Line and Regression Curve for x on y, or M.A., on 'Arithmetic Problems' (National A, #1), for Miscellaneous Sampling a, Grades 5-7.*

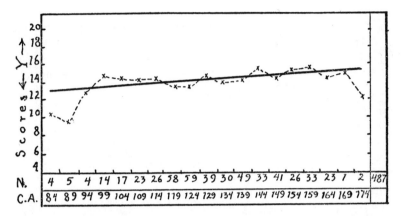

FIG. 7. *Regression Line and Regression Curve for y on x, or 'Arithmetic Problems' (National A, #1) on C.A., for Composite of All Samplings, Grades 3-7. 487 Cases.*

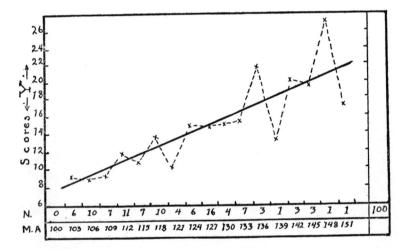

FIG. 8. *Regression Line and Regression Curve for y on x, or 'Arithmetic Problems' (National A, #1) on M.A., for Miscellaneous Sampling β, Grades 3-4.*

1. *The Case for the Range Covered by Samplings in Grades 5-7, Richmond and Monessen*

Upon an examination of Figures 1-5 one does not find sufficient evidence to cause him to think that 'arithmetic problems' is distinctly more applicable to one level of mental age than to another. The one diagram given for C.A. does not show the assumption of linearity of regression to be unreasonable in that case, and this is believed to be a fair sample of all the distributions where C.A. and sub-test scores are the variables. Admittedly no evidence has been given the reader to prove that the distributions selected for detailed study show greater tendencies than those for any other sub-tests to display a form other than rectilinear. But in view of the infeasibility of reproducing here all the distributions, we will probably be pardoned for simply claiming that this appears to be true. We argue thus: The curves through the means of the arrays diverged in one general direction from the respective regression lines to a greater degree in these distributions than in any others; but these distributions show these sub-tests to be about as applicable to one part of the range as to another; therefore all the sub-tests here studied may be considered as about as applicable to one part of this range as to another. This, of course, carries with it the idea that for practical purposes the ranks assigned to the sub-tests apply, in general, not only to the whole range studied (Grades 5-7), but to the smaller divisions of it as well.

2. *The Case for Range Covered by Samplings in Grades 3-7*

An illustration of the danger of applying the obtained K-indices to too wide a range.—Let it be emphasized that the figures upon which the above statements have been made are taken from ranges of ages and grades that are by no means unlimited. If the variabilities in M.A. and in C.A. had been larger, and if pupils in Grades 3-7 had been grouped together instead of being dealt with separately in three groups, we cannot say with certainty what the facts concerning the applicability of the product-moment formula would have been. In any case where the K-index obtained for the sampling in Grades 3-4 is not appreciably different from that obtained in the other samplings, we have no particular reason to doubt that the sub-test is as amenable to treatment by the correlation method at one level as at another of the entire range represented by all three samplings. However, if there are distinct discrepancies between the indices, one possible explanation lies in the difference in the applicability of the product-moment method at different levels. For a practical illustration of the point, note the following diagram (Fig. 9) which represents the regression line b_{yx} and the broken line for η_{yx} based upon a correlation table for 'arithmetic problems' (National A, #1) versus

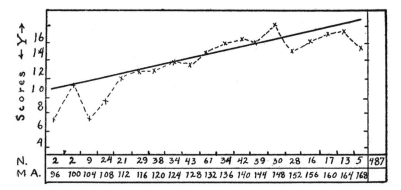

| N. | 2 | 2 | 9 | 24 | 21 | 29 | 38 | 34 | 43 | 61 | 34 | 42 | 39 | 30 | 28 | 16 | 17 | 13 | 5 | 487 |
| M.A. | 96 | 100 | 104 | 108 | 112 | 116 | 120 | 124 | 128 | 132 | 136 | 140 | 144 | 148 | 152 | 156 | 160 | 164 | 168 | |

Fig. 9.   *Regression Line and Regression Curve for y on x, or 'Arithmetic Problems' (National A, #1) on M.A., for Composite of All Samplings, Grades 3-7.   487 Cases.*

mental age for all 487 children of the three samplings. Consider also in this connection Figure 8.

As far as our data go, it appears that if we had no cases above 153 M.A., as is the case in Miscellaneous sampling β, Grades 3-4, the line b_{yx} would become more steep, approaching more closely the general trend of the line passing through the actual means of the arrays in that area. Is it surprising that for any sampling the greater the proportion of cases above M.A. of 151, the lower the r? Consider the r_{s-MA} for each of the three samplings:

In Miscellaneous β,
     Grades 3-4: where   1% of the cases were above 151, $r = .623$
In Richmond,
     Grade 5A: where   3% of the cases were above 151, $r = .431$
In Miscellaneous α,
     Grades 5-7: where   37% of the cases were above 151, $r = .315$

Moreover, since in the 3-4 grade sampling 51 per cent of the cases were below 121 M.A., another possible reason is suggested by the diagram as to why the b_{yx} line may be more steep in this sampling than in either of the other two.

Conclusions from Cases 1 and 2

Mention of the above points—together with the fact that will be presented later to the effect that the combined distribution departs more from rectilinearity than any single distribution—is made not in the hope of establishing anything of value outside the main line of this study, but as an illustration of the danger of applying uncritically the K-indices assigned in one connection to ranges wider than those upon which the calculations were based. It is not thought that the facts for this one sub-test are typical of what would be found for the others. From an inspection of all the scatter diagrams, we think an extreme case has been selected, but it points out the problem, and that is all we have in mind here. The upshot of the whole matter, as far as the diagrams show, is that a sub-test may be used over a certain range without overtaxing very much the assumption of linearity of regression; but over other ranges the general trend of the line through the means of the arrays may diverge from that of the regression lines to such an extent as to indicate that the sub-test is not adapted to the task of testing mentality equally well at all levels. Though an extreme case has been chosen, the fact that even one sub-test shows such a tendency makes it worthy of consideration. These diagrams at least serve the purpose of emphasizing the fact that in evaluating sub-tests attention must be given to the ranges in which they are to be used.

PART II

THE ASSUMPTION OF LINEARITY OF REGRESSION AS APPLIED TO ONE TYPE OF SUB-TEST

The point that has just been shown by diagrams, to the effect that the general trend of lines through means of the arrays may diverge from the respective regression lines more at one point of the range than at another, is an important one; but unfortunately we have been unable to express the results mathematically. Closely allied with this problem is another the results for which we shall present mathematically with the hope that the two attacks may supplement each other. The plan here is to determine how much the correlation ratios differ from the coefficients of correlation for whole distributions. The two attacks appear on the surface quite unrelated to each other, for the former deals with inspection of trends for *parts* of the distribution; the latter with trends for the whole distribution. But since the distribution of all cases for Grades 3-7 is available as a whole and also in the three samplings, the second method may show by its comparison of trends for whole distributions facts similar to those shown by the first in its comparison of trends for parts of distributions.

In following this mode of attack occasion will be offered to test the distributions for linearity of regression. For this purpose the Blakeman Formula [1] will be employed. Our number of cases, divided as they are among three groups, is small for use in this formula. But so far as our data go the following table gives the facts for 'arithmetic problems' as this sub-test occurs in the three different tests. The results obtained by the formula should be less than 2.5 if the distribution is to be considered rectilinear.

TABLE X

r AND η AND THE RESULTS ON THE BLAKEMAN FORMULA FOR 'ARITHMETIC PROBLEMS' *vs.* M.A.

Tests and Sub-Tests	Richmond, Grade 5A					Miscellaneous *a*, Gr. 5-7				
	r	η_{xy}	η_{yx}	BF_{xy}	BF_{yx}	*r*	η_{xy}	η_{yx}	BF_{xy}	BF_{yx}
Nat. A., ‡1 Arith. Prob.	.431	.516	.547	3.04	3.61	.315	.480	.508	3.59	3.95
Otis, ‡5 Arith. Prob.	.518	.547	.582	1.88	2.84	.454	.495	.584	1.95	3.64
Hag., ‡2 Arith. Prob.	.479	.. *	.581	...	3.52	.505	...	.623	...	3.62

* The η_{xy} for Haggerty Delta 2, sub-test ‡2, was not worked because we were convinced both by the inspection of the distribution and by the comparison of each pair of η's in this table that this η_{xy} would not be larger than the η_{yx}, and since we are interested chiefly in maximum figures here, this ratio would have been of little value.

Is the assumption of linearity of regression justifiable for ranges in grades, mental ages and chronological ages, such as have been used in the three samplings?—From the figures given

[1] $\dfrac{\sqrt{N}}{.67449} \cdot \tfrac{1}{2}\sqrt{\eta^2 - r^2} < 2.5.$ Blakeman, J., *Biometrika*, IV, p. 349. Quoted by Brown and Thomson, *The Essentials of Mental Measurement*, p. 113.

in Table X it will be observed that in a strict sense we are not justified in assuming linearity of regression in several of the above distributions, and therefore not justified in the use of the product-moment method. This is a criticism of our whole procedure. Rugg (1917, p. 283) has expressed well the practical difficulty that we face here. He says: "To the writer's knowledge no published analysis has been made of educational distributions which have used both the product-moment and the correlation ratio methods. Thus little comparative data are available for use at this point. We are interested to know: Under what conditions can we use the product-moment formula?" The difficulty is not that the statisticians have not supplied us with sufficient methods for testing for linearity, but the practical one of what to do when the regression lines of our distributions do not approach linearity closely enough to satisfy the Blakeman criterion, but do not depart from it enough to assume the form of any defined type of mathematical curve. We must have some method by which the values of one variable can be predicted from known values of the other or others. Therefore, just how serious this criticism of our procedure is the reader will have to decide for himself. In making his decision he will not forget (1) that this sub-test, as it occurred in the three examinations, was selected because it appeared to be the one which showed the least tendency toward fulfilling the conditions of linearity of regression; and (2) that this criticism may be launched against the whole method of test construction. In correlating a sub-test against mental age, we are but making the same assumptions as were made by the authors who included these component tests in their examinations.[1]

[1] In this connection we are reminded of the views expressed by Ruml, Kelley, and Terman in 1920-1921. Dr. Ruml's ideas may be fairly represented by the following quotations: "If we were approaching the field without too definite statistical prejudices, I am inclined to think that we should question before we got very far the implications of the assumption of linear regressions between test performance and general intelligence. . . . Consider any test you please, it is fairly obvious that for certain ranges, either extremely high or extremely low, differences in intelligence will not be paralleled by differences in test performances." Ruml, B., "The Need for an Examination of Certain Hypotheses in Mental Tests," *Journal of Philosophy, Psychology, and Scientific Methods* (1920), Vol. 17, pp. 57-61.
In reply to this article, Kelley and Terman argued, in part, as follows: "It is more nearly in accord with the facts to say that rectilinear regressions have been found than to say that they have been assumed. . . . Not a single regression sufficiently non-rectilinear to permit determination of its type was found by Dr. Kelley in an extended treatment of the results

Though the results on the Blakeman formula are larger in the Miscellaneous sampling α in every case than those in Richmond, the differences do not appear to be large enough to cause one to think that the correlation method is much more applicable to the Richmond than to the Miscellaneous data. This is rather important, even though we are aware that results on these three sub-tests are too few for generalization. But so far as they go, they would tend to disprove any claim that differences found to exist between Richmond and Miscellaneous samplings are due to differences in the applicability of the correlation method in the two cases. Moreover, looking at the same thing from a slightly different angle, we see in Table X that facts portrayed by the correlation ratios are largely the same as shown by the r's. Note, for example, the relative position assigned to each of the sub-tests by the r's and by the η's in the Richmond and in the Miscellaneous α samplings. Second, compare Richmond and Miscellaneous α data column for column. To be sure, the η's are always higher than the r's, but relative standing is what counts here. To the extent that conclusions based on r's are supported by conclusions based on η's it would seem that, though the r method may not be applicable in the strictest sense of statistical theory, its use may be defended on practical grounds.

It is admitted that there is a weakness in this defense of the correlation method on practical grounds. The weakness lies in the fact that once the method is used in distributions to which it does not strictly apply mathematically, the question then is not, Are we justified in using the method? but rather, How much error are we causing by employing it? How much error shall we excuse on practical grounds? The following section will give practical consideration to these questions.

With wider ranges would the assumption of linearity of regression be justifiable?—When a comparison is made in Table XI between the results based on all samplings combined and the re-

of twenty-two different serial groups of children and various kinds of criteria in connection with work on the National Intelligence Scale. . . . Surely, with all the scatter diagrams that have been published in the last ten years, it devolves upon the critic to point to specific situations where material error in conclusions has resulted from the assumption of recti-linearity." Kelley, Truman, L. and Terman, Lewis M., "Dr. Ruml's Criticism of Mental Test Methods," *The Journal of Philosophy* (1921), Vol. 18, pp. 459-65.

spective results for each of the samplings separately, significant differences occur.

TABLE XI

SHOWING r, η, AND RESULTS ON THE BLAKEMAN FORMULA FOR 'ARITHMETIC PROBLEMS' (NAT. A, #1) VERSUS M.A. AND C.A. FOR THE THREE SAMPLINGS AND FOR A COMPOSITE OF THESE THREE

Sampling	Grade	No.	Sub-test vs. M.A.			Sub-test vs. C.A.		
			r	η_{yx}	BF_{yx}	r	η_{yx}	BF_{yx}
Richmond	5A	208	+ .431	.547	3.61	− .079	....	....
Miscellaneous α	5-7	179	+ .315	.508	3.95	+ .109	....	....
Miscellaneous β	3-4	100	+ .623	.688	2.17	− .040	....	....
Composite	3-7	487	+ .352	.512	6.08	+ .125	.212	2.80

Notice especially the low result for r and the high result for Blakeman Formula in Miscellaneous α (Grades 5-7); the high r and the low figure for BF for Miscellaneous β and the unusually high results for BF in the composite of all samplings. These figures indicate rather conclusively that a sub-test may show some special adaptability to particular ranges.

A K-index would have little meaning when applied to a sub-test whose distribution departed so much from rectilinearity as to show a result of 6.08 in the Blakeman Formula. In such a case it would seem that the K-indices based on smaller ranges than those for the total of the 487 cases would be of more practical service for evaluating sub-tests. If we wish to select a sub-test for use in the sixth grade, for example, where we expect the variability in M.A. and C.A. to be not greater than that in the Richmond or Miscellaneous α samplings, we have implied in a previous paragraph that we would consider the K-indices of the two samplings comparable, and combine them in order to get the best approximation to the true K-index. But if we were called upon to select component tests for an examination to be used in the fourth grade, where the variability in M.A. and C.A. was not greater than in Miscellaneous β, we would be inclined to give more consideration to the sub-test 'arithmetic problems' than the K-indices of the two higher-grade samplings or that of the composite of all samplings would justify. That is, the K-index resulting from the correlations obtained in the area where the sub-test is to be used should receive considerable weight. If the task upon us were the selection, according to our data, of the best sub-test for use in Grades 3 to 7, where the variability in M.A. and C.A. was similar to that obtained in the composite distribution, we would, of course, select those sub-tests whose K-indices placed them high in all three samplings; but we would be very cautious about selecting a sub-test which showed a high rank in both Richmond and Miscellaneous α (Grades 5-7), but a low one in Miscellaneous β, (Grades 3-4), or vice versa. A comparison between the η's and the $r's$, together with an inspection of the scatter diagrams, should indicate in doubtful cases whether a distribution was showing marked tendencies over certain areas to be non-rectilinear.

The Fact Emphasized in This Chapter as One Possible Explanation for Lack of Agreement Among K-indices

The point concerning the difference in the applicability of the product-moment method at various levels of the range has bearing on the explanation of the different K-indices obtained for a sub-test in various samplings. Other possible reasons for differences are: nature of the sampling, and errors of measurement. Any one who is interested in accounting for differences in the correlation coefficients or K-indices obtained for sub-tests of the *same type* which occur in different examinations (such as 'arithmetic problems' in three examinations, 'analogies' in two examinations, 'general information' in two) will add to these possible explanations the fact that differences in the content as well as in the form of a sub-test are very important. The fact that the author of an examination selects good types of sub-tests is obviously no guarantee that he will make a good examination, because he may include poor material in the construction of each sub-test.

The general topic of explaining the differences in ranks or K-indices obtained for the same type of sub-test in different samplings and in different tests might seem at first an attractive and promising one, and one to which some attention should be given here. However, the thoughts presented might partake too much of the appearance of unwarranted excuse-making. We divided our data into three groups, to be treated separately, with the expectation that differences would occur and that the unreliability of our K-indices would be shown by these discrepancies. To attempt to explain at this point differences found, might give the impression that we were taking the obtained K-indices too seriously; that we thought that from each of our samplings we had obtained a very reliable K-index for each sub-test and that where discrepancies occurred an explanation was in order. A less enthusiastic attitude is taken. If the K-indices for a sub-test are about the same for all three samplings, we assume that the obtained K-indices are about correct; if they disagree we make a guess that the true K-index is somewhere within the range represented—though even this might not be true. This interpretation, it seems to the writer, is all that is justified and all that is necessary to establish the major point of this study, viz., that sub-tests can be ranked on the basis of how well they measure mental maturity irrespective of factors other than native brightness. Both the ranks and the K-indices are merely convenient devices for summarization. The K-index of a given sub-test is subject to the errors of sampling and mis-measurement. Besides, the K-index of a given sub-test is dependent upon the excellence of the other component tests because the other sub-tests, together with this one, determined the M.A. against which the sub-test is correlated. If we change the sub-tests in the total battery, we shall most likely change the M.A. which was part of our original criterion. With the evidence given to the effect that differences in the applicability of the product-moment method to component tests at various levels may account for discrepancies in K-indices, together with an enumeration of other causes that might contribute toward such differences, we are content to leave the matter, deeming that little of value to the central point under investigation would result from an attempted explanation of each difference.

Summary.—It has been the main purpose of this chapter (1) to show, by detailed study of one type of sub-test, that a sub-test may be a better measure of intelligence at one area of a distribution than at another, and (2) to show the bearing of this on the obtained ranks and K-indices. The general method employed was to determine how much the distributions departed from rectilinearity of regression. To accomplish this two devices were used: (1) an inspectional method which roughly indicated how much the trend of the line through the actual means of the arrays diverged from the regression line at various *parts* of a given correlation table; (2) a more exact method involving the use of the correlation ratio and the Blakeman Formula by which the departure from rectilinearity could be shown for a whole distribution. As far as the main issues were concerned, both methods showed the same results, but the advantage of the former was that those distributions which showed marked tendencies to be non-rectilinear could be chosen readily for detailed study. The advantage of the second was mathematical accuracy. The type of sub-test which showed the strongest tendency toward non-rectilinearity was chosen by the former method for minute study. It was 'arithmetic problems'. Even in the case of this sub-test the distributions of this study, presented separately as they are for the three samplings, do not seem to depart from rectilinearity enough to invalidate our general results. However, if one wishes to apply the figures obtained here to other ranges of grades and ages than we have employed or to wider ranges than we have used, he is cautioned not to place too much faith in our r's or any figures based on these, if he has reason to believe that the sub-test is a better measure of intelligence at one level than at another. The suspicion of this may be aroused by large discrepancies between K-indices obtained at different levels. However, such discrepancies do not prove that the distributions are non-rectilinear, because other causes which are enumerated may account for these differences. Therefore, to separate these latter causes from the matter of non-rectilinearity of distribution, the methods employed in this study may be valuable.

CHAPTER V

EFFECT OF C.A. AND OTHER FACTORS AS SHOWN BY FIVE HIGHEST AND FIVE LOWEST SUB-TESTS

In Chapter III the sub-tests were ranked in the order of excellence on the basis of how near each one approached a certain standard. It will be recalled that this standard was that that sub-test was best whose correlation with M.A.—C.A. constant—was nearest $+$ 1.00, and whose correlation with C.A.—M.A. constant—was nearest 0.[1] The success with which these sub-tests were ranked can be studied by comparing the properties of some of those which ranked high with some which ranked low. It was decided to combine the highest five sub-tests into a sort of 'all star' team, and the lowest five into another imaginary battery. There were no very important reasons for selecting five rather than any other number. The upper five and lower five were rather naturally divided off from the rest by a somewhat remarkable agreement among the three rankings as to which were the highest and lowest five. Only two rankings out of the fifteen assigned to the sub-tests called 'five highest' placed any of these outside of the upper five. Likewise only two rankings out of the fifteen would indicate that any of the five lowest do not belong to this group. There would not be so great an agreement among the rankings as to which were the highest or lowest four, or the

[1] It was pointed out that, in the case of even one sub-test, zero would appear as a small minus quantity, due to the sub-test's being included in the battery. On account of the difficulty of working out the slight correction necessary, and the fact that for practical purposes of ranking the sub-tests in this study it was not especially needed, this series of partial r's was computed without the correction. When we try to combine five sub-tests, we have the same problem again. We know that since five sub-tests are being correlated against the battery which includes the five, the real zero correlation between the five highest sub-tests and C.A.—M.A. constant—will appear as a noticeably high negative value. Again, for practical purposes, however, it is not necessary to work out the correction. We are certain that any plus values obtained for this partial will show that chronological age is being measured to an undesirable degree. The figures will be such as to show clearly one thing or the other, and will not hinge upon the correction.

highest or lowest six. Another consideration which led to the selection of five was that, since two of our tests were composed of five sub-tests each and another was composed of six, the imaginary battery of five would be equal, as far as the number of sub-tests was concerned, to two of the real tests and closely similar to a third.

TABLE XII

THE HIGHEST FIVE SUB-TESTS AND THE LOWEST FIVE, TOGETHER WITH THEIR RANKS

Test	Sub-Test	Ranks			
		Rich.	Misc. α	Misc. β	Comb.
Highest Haggerty, Delta 2..	#6, Information	1	2	1	1
National A	#2, Sent. Completion	5	1	2	2
National, Scale B...	#2, Information	3	3	8	3
Otis Adv. Exam....	#7, Analogies	4	5	..	4
National, Scale A...	#3, Logical Selection	2	12	5	5
Lowest National, Scale B...	#5, Visual Comparison	26	26	24	26
National, Scale A...	#5, Symbol Digit	24	24	21	25
National, Scale B...	#1, Fund. Arithmetic	25	25	13	24
Haggerty, Delta 2..	#3, Picture Completion	23	23	20	23
National, Scale A...	#1, Prob. Arithmetic	22	22	7	22

There are two matters in particular upon which this comparison of five highest and five lowest sub-tests should shed light: first, the reason for treating three sets of data separately in this study; second, the reasons for believing this method of selecting sub-tests dependent upon C.A. will be of any value for selecting sub-tests which depend upon other factors irrelevant to brightness. These, together with the more obvious purpose of showing the relative excellence of the best five and the worst five when compared with the double criterion, are all that we have in mind. We do not claim the imaginary battery to be a real test and the best one that could be selected from the twenty-six component tests. The construction of a mental test is more than the selecting of sub-tests which show high correlations with mental ages which we consider reliable—or the selecting of sub-tests which correlate high with mental ages and low with chronological ages, if the criterion of this study is accepted. The combining of component tests into a team is an important aspect of test construction, and demands that we compute, in addition to the correlation between each sub-test and mental age, the correlation existing among the various sub-tests, and the optimum weight for each sub-test. But since the writer has no intention of making a new test, and has here only one purpose in view, viz., the study of a composite based upon the five highest sub-tests and of one based on the five lowest, he feels justified in making a plain summation of the scores on the five highest component tests, which will be called five highest (5H or H), and a similar summation for the five lowest (5L or L).

Tables XIII and XIV show interesting facts concerning the five best or highest, and five worst or lowest sub-tests. In Table XIII the first four partials will probably be of most significance, but all correlations are included for the sake of completeness. Since there are four variables, partials with two variables constant could have been computed, but it seems that nothing of value would have been shown by such partials.

$r_{MA-H.CA}$ (of Table XIII).—The total r_{MA-H} is high for both Richmond and Miscellaneous α, and it is practically identical in the two samplings. If we should try to conclude anything from the fact that these figures are so nearly the same, it would be that apparently it makes little difference upon the correlation between group mental age and five highest sub-tests, whether educational

TABLE XIII

TOTAL AND PARTIAL CORRELATIONS FOR FIVE HIGHEST AND FIVE LOWEST SUB-TESTS FOR RICHMOND, GRADE 5A, AND MISCELLANEOUS α, GRADES 5-7

	Richmond	Miscellaneous α
r_{MA-H}	+ .890	+ .893
r_{MA-L}	+ .631	+ .199
r_{H-L}	+ .440	+ .071
r_{H-CA}	− .198	− .343
r_{L-CA}	− .056	+ .413
r_{MA-CA}	− .210	− .280
$r_{MA-H.CA}$	+ .885	+ .885
$r_{MA-L.CA}$	+ .644	+ .360
$r_{H-CA.MA}$	− .025	− .215
$r_{L-CA.MA}$	+ .101	+ .498
$r_{MA-H.L}$	+ .878	+ .898
$r_{MA-L.H}$	+ .584	+ .303
$r_{L-H.MA}$	− .342	− .243
$r_{H-CA.L}$	− .193	− .410
$r_{L-CA.H}$	+ .035	+ .467
$r_{H-L.CA}$	+ .439	+ .249
$r_{MA-CA.H}$	− .076	+ .061
$r_{MA-CA.L}$	− .226	− .405

opportunities for sub-groups in the total sampling are closely similar, as in Richmond, or widely different, as in Miscellaneous α. This conclusion is supported by the partial $r_{MA-H.CA}$, which happens to be identical for the two sets of data ($+ .885$), and by the regressions X_{MA} of the group, $MA.H.CA$. Moreover, the fact that the partial is so slightly different from the total correlation

TABLE XIV

PARTIAL REGRESSION EQUATIONS FOR RICHMOND, GRADE 5A, AND MISCELLANEOUS α, GRADES 5-7. EQUATIONS GROUPED ACCORDING TO THE VARIABLES CONCERNED

Richmond	Miscellaneous α
GROUP MA.H.CA	
$X_{MA} = + 94.9 + .557X_H - .034X_{CA}$	$X_{MA} = + 86.6 + .570X_H + .029X_{CA}$
$X_H = - 108.2 + 1.407X_{MA} - .018X_{CA}$	$X_H = - 82.1 + 1.375X_{MA} - .157X_{CA}$
$X_{CA} = + 158.0 - .158X_{MA} - .036X_H$	$X_{CA} = + 152.9 + .129X_{MA} - .293X_H$
GROUP MA.L.CA	
$X_{MA} = + 96.1 - .165X_{CA} + .700X$	$X_{MA} = + 173.5 - .436X_{CA} + .353X_L$
$X_{CA} = + 162.6 - .309X_{MA} + .150X_L$	$X_{CA} = + 154.7 - .373X_{MA} + .457X_L$
$X_L = - 3.4 + .592X_{MA} + .068X_{CA}$	$X_L = - 36.0 + .364X_{MA} + .542X_{CA}$
GROUP MA.H.L	
$X_{MA} = + 68.4 + .478X_H + .332X_L$	$X_{MA} = + 79.9 + .557X_H + .128X_L$
$X_H = - 108.0 + 1.615X_{MA} - .358X_L$	$X_H = - 99.2 + 1.446X_{MA} - .166X_L$
$X_L = - 26.8 + 1.025X_{MA} - .327X_H$	$X_L = + 25.3 + .712X_{MA} - .356X_H$
GROUP CA.H.L	
$X_{CA} = + 141.2 - .142X_H + .045X_L$	$X_{CA} = + 127.0 - .239X_H + .418X_L$
$X_H = + 46.8 - .262X_{CA} + .768X_L$	$X_H = + 168.4 - .701X_{CA} + .381X_L$
$X_L = + 65.0 + .027X_{CA} + .207X_H$	$X_L = + 4.1 + .523X_{CA} + .162X_H$

is evidence that the highest sub-tests are very little affected by changes in chronological age.

$r_{MA-L.CA}$ —In contrast with $r_{MA-H.CA}$, examine the partial $r_{MA-L.CA}$ for Richmond and Miscellaneous α. When Richmond children of the same chronological age are studied, there is a noticeable correlation between mental age and the five lowest sub-tests ($r_{MA-L.CA} = + .644$); but there is a relatively low correlation for those of Miscellaneous α ($r_{MA-L.CA} = + .360$). The regressions for X_{MA} of the group $MA.L.CA$ are helpful here. These figures point to the conclusion that in cases where educational opportunities are fairly equal, there is a considerably higher correlation remaining between the five lowest sub-tests and the group mental ages, after the effect of C.A. is removed, than in those cases where such opportunities are widely different.

Obviously, in attempting to interpret these figures we must not overlook the fact that the five lowest sub-tests form roughly $\frac{5}{26}$ of the battery by which the mental age was determined.[1] In terms of correlation, this means that the coefficient of correlation between mental age and the five lowest sub-tests, due solely to the fact of the presence of five common elements, is $+ .439$. Thus it seems that the five lowest sub-tests are contributing nothing toward the measurement of group mental age for a sampling of this population like that of Miscellaneous α. In fact, for constant C.A., the total scores on the five lowest sub-tests do not agree with the total scores of the battery which includes these five as well as five scores given at random would. According to the figures for the Richmond sampling, the lowest sub-tests seem to be contributing something toward the measurement of M.A. In none of the Richmond partials do we find a figure lower than that of the rough calculation of agreement we should expect due to common scores. This difference between the facts for Richmond and Miscellaneous α is significant, as will be shown later, in indicating that these sub-tests tend to impair a measure of mental age by including not only chronological age but other factors irrelevant to brightness. But the main point here is that there is a real difference between the correlation of five highest sub-tests with M.A.—C.A. constant—and five lowest sub-tests with M.A.—C.A. constant. Since this is true in dissimilar types of sampling of the population, and since there is nothing in the manner in which our mental ages were determined that would account for this, the difference between the obtained correlations must point to a real difference between the two sets of sub-tests.

$r_{H-CA.MA}$—But let us see how the two sets are related to C.A. The partial $r_{H-CA.MA}$ is negative for both Richmond and Miscellaneous α. Since the variability of chronological age and the variability in other factors irrelevant to brightness which act like chronological age are greater in Miscellaneous α than in Richmond, we are not surprised to see the higher negative correlation in the case of the former. But the main point is that both are so near real zero. These two figures are significant in that they show that the five highest component tests are influenced little, if any, by

[1] For calculation of this, see p. 70.

chronological age. This is the same fact that was shown from another angle in a previous paragraph. (See p. 57.)

$r_{L-CA.MA}$—In contrast with the r just mentioned, consider $r_{L-CA.MA}$ of $+ .101$ for Richmond, and of $+ .498$ for Miscellaneous α. There seems to be no doubt that the five lowest sub-tests are measuring factors which are dependent upon chronological age; and in view of the unusually high correlation, relatively, for the Miscellaneous sampling, it seems clear that other factors acting like chronological age are especially potent in these measurements. Examine the regression equation X_{CA} of $MA.L.CA$ for Richmond and Miscellaneous α for further details about this relationship.

These few facts are so plain that they cannot be misunderstood; their practical bearing on mental measurement is of such importance that it cannot be ignored. If two children of the same group mental age differ a great deal in chronological age, educational opportunities, or both, then the older one, and the one with the greater opportunities to learn, will get a higher score on the five lowest sub-tests than would the younger child or the one whose opportunities have been more limited. But how can they have the same mental age if their scores on these sub-tests, which help to determine mental age, are different? **Only by virtue of the fact that all the sub-tests are not like these.** The younger child makes up for this loss on other component tests which are more a measure of native brightness. But the great question still remains as to whether the mental ages of the two children should be equal, because the extra score obtained by one child as a result of having lived in the world for a longer period, or among richer surroundings, or both, has never been deducted. According to the reasoning of this study, this extra score is an increment which always favors the older child, or the one with better environment. As a result, a mental age of 10 for an eight-year-old child and a mental age of 10 for a twelve-year-old child are, in reality, not the same mental ages at all.

In view of the fact that both total and partial correlations are presented in Table XIII, it might prove interesting to some to attempt to draw some conclusion from a comparison between a partial and the total correlation from which it is taken. This would be the more interesting in that we have three degrees of selection for the variable C.A. We have very mild selection in the Miscellaneous α sampling; but it is a selection nevertheless, because we could not claim that we have a fair sampling of all the population between ages 6 and 16, for example, in Grades 5-8 inclusive, nor could we claim that we have a fair selection, from the best to the worst, in educational opportunities, though this group is very heterogeneous in the latter respect. In Richmond the selection is mild. In the partials it is rigorous. In view of what has just been said, all of the correlations must be considered as partials, but by reference to partials in this study we mean those which are expressed in partial correlation form. And even one set of these, namely, the Richmond partials, is more strictly a group of partials than those of Miscellaneous α, if the other irrelevant factors are to be grouped with C.A. As a result of these several degrees of selection for the variable C.A., it would be interesting to compare correlation coefficients. Especially is one tempted to try to conclude, from a consideration of total and partial correlations, something concerning the common elements of M.A. in the five highest and the five lowest sub-tests. The common elements of M.A. existing between chronological age and the five lowest sub-tests is another fertile field for speculation. The writer has, for amusement, given some time to trying various hypotheses of common elements upon the figures of Tables XIII and XIV. But such hypotheses cannot be tested easily. We are subjected to two dangerous fallacies in attempting to interpret the facts of Table XIII further than has already been done. The first is that of using the facts upon which a hypothesis is based, to prove the hypothesis. A second fallacy, more common and more subtle, is that involved in attempting to determine, from coefficients of partial correlation, the structural relationships existing among elements or factors which compose the related variables. Dr. Godfrey Thomson[1] has shown conclusively that a given partial correlation may be consistent with any one of several structural arrangements of the factors constituting the variables.

These statements would not invalidate what has been said in a previous paragraph (see discussion of $r_{MA-L.CA}$) about common elements existing between the five lowest sub-tests and the twenty-six sub-tests constituting the entire battery. The elements re-

[1] Brown and Thomson (1921), *The Essentials of Mental Measurement,* pp. 139-45.

ferred to in that connection as common elements are known to be such. In the Appendix of this study a section will be given to the calculation of the coefficient of correlation where we know common elements to exist, and occasion will be offered to show by illustration how in one case we have sufficient knowledge of the variables to be justified in employing a simple formula for detecting the amount of correlation due to common elements, while in the other case such knowledge is not available.

VALUE OF TREATING DIFFERENT SAMPLINGS OF THE POPULATION SEPARATELY

It may seem unusual that a justification for the procedure of computing the results for several samplings separately is reserved until this point, but it was desired that the wisdom of the method should be judged from the facts which it disclosed. All the facts had not been presented until this page was reached and therefore the justification on the basis of actual facts had to be delayed.

(1) *Treating samplings separately, together with the method of working with highest and lowest items, focalizes attention on significant differences.*—It has become clear from an examination of the figures for Richmond and Miscellaneous α that real differences exist. Of course, differences between Richmond and Miscellaneous α correlations were noticed when dealing with the individual sub-tests. But the facts based on single sub-tests gave no definite impression, because it was felt that these might be due to errors such as might come from having different examiners in the various samplings, to errors of scoring, to differences among pupils in familiarity with tests, etc. But when scores based on five component tests selected out of the twenty-six show very marked differences from scores based on five others, it seems that there must be real causes operating, and not merely chance inaccuracies. Especially is this true since we would expect the differences due to the chance inaccuracies to grow less as the number of sub-tests upon which the figures are based is increased. It is evident that these discrepancies due to the nature of the sampling would not have been discovered if we had not treated separately more than one set of data, however typical and diversified the sampling might have been. In order to emphasize these discrepancies, a brief summary will be given of the differ-

ences in the nature of two of the samplings, and figures will be selected from Table XIII to show differences in the results based upon these samplings.

First, let us review the outstanding differences between the Richmond and the Miscellaneous α samplings. The Richmond material is based on school children of the first half of the fifth grade in one city; the Miscellaneous α data, on pupils of grades five to seven, inclusive, of three different towns or cities. In the Richmond sampling there are no pupils of foreign parentage; practically all of the pupils in the other sampling were born in America, and all of them speak English, but many of them hear little English spoken in the homes. Though it is difficult to establish the point, it is felt definitely that the social status of the Richmond group is not so varied as that of the Miscellaneous α group. That is, the range is not so wide, and there is a closer clustering around the average.

Keeping in mind the differences in the nature of the samplings, let us select the most significant coefficients of correlation from the two samplings, for the purpose of comparison.

	Richmond	Miscellaneous α
r_{CA-L}	— .056	+ .413
$r_{CA-L.MA}$	+ .101	+ .498
r_{MA-L}	+ .631	+ .199
$r_{MA-L.CA}$	+ .644	+ .360
r_{CA-H}	— .198	— .343
$r_{CA-H.MA}$	— .025	— .215
r_{MA-H}	+ .890	+ .893
$r_{MA-H.CA}$	+ .885	+ .885

Some comments on the meaning of these figures and of the differences existing between the two columns were made in the last section; others will be made in the following one. However, let it suffice here to emphasize the point that one value of our method is that it points out facts which deserve **explanation.**

(2) *Treating samplings separately throws light on other factors than C.A. which may be irrelevant to brightness.*—Not only does the treating of the several dissimilar samplings of the population separately make possible a clear presentation of the effect that sampling has on these correlations, but it makes possible a more accurate and extensive interpretation of the *r*'s. Throughout our discussion thus far we have referred to the effects of C.A., or of *other factors which act like C.A.* No justification has been made

for this last clause. At this point we are ready to extend our hypothesis so as to take some account of factors other than C.A. which are irrelevant to brightness.

Assume that one's chances to learn can be divided into length of life (pure C.A.), and richness of contacts (environmental opportunities). Then if these two can be separated, we may gain important information about both factors. See next page for an attempt at a logical analysis. Let us suppose that any sub-test that is largely dependent upon C.A. is also largely dependent on other factors of opportunity. Since these sub-tests have been included in some of our best intelligence tests, there must be some reason for including them. Let us suppose they measure M.A. fairly well so long as the variability in opportunities is not wide. From these premises we should argue that where there is a wide range of difference in opportunities, both in length of life and in richness of life, much of the correlation between such sub-tests and group M.A. might be traceable to these facts which are not matters of brightness at all. On the other hand, for a group where opportunities to learn were fairly constant, such sub-tests would measure brightness to the extent that they were able, and would have little opportunity to measure factors irrelevant to brightness. Such factors, in other words, would be included in the latter case to only a slight extent in either group M.A. or the five lowest sub-tests.

But how do the facts accord with these suppositions? The partial $r_{MA\text{-}L.CA}$ of $+.644$ for Richmond and of $+.360$ for Miscellaneous α are consistent with them, because the population in Richmond is more homogeneous in educational opportunities. In other words, this means that where educational opportunities are nearer constant,—that is, where C.A. becomes more exclusively a measure of length of life,—the correlation between five lowest sub-tests and group mental age is considerably higher. Also the partial $r_{CA\text{-}L.MA}$, which is $+.101$ for Richmond and $+.498$ for Miscellaneous α, lends support to the hypothesis. Interpreted in terms of our hypothesis, this means that for constant mental age the relation between five lowest sub-tests and C.A. is larger where C.A. includes, to the greater degree, both extent of life (pure C.A.), and intensity of living (richness of opportunities).

Following the same reasoning, we should expect the five highest sub-tests to be largely independent of C.A. and other factors

AN ATTEMPTED ANALYSIS OF FACTORS UNDERLYING VARIOUS SUB-TEST SCORES

How Many and How Difficult Things an Individual Can Do } will depend upon {

1. Native Mental Ability, or Brightness
2. Opportunities to Learn } will depend upon {
   (a) Length of Life, Pure C.A., or Extent of Living
   (b) Environmental Factors, Richness of Contacts, or Intensity of Living

representing opportunities, and to deal more strictly with pure M.A. It should be said here that we do not wish to complicate matters by introducing a new and utopian term, when we refer to pure mental age. Specifically, we mean the nearest approach that we have to a measure which favors neither the old nor the young, neither the child with broad opportunities to learn nor the one with narrow opportunities.[1] We find the correlation between M.A. and five highest—C.A. constant—to be $+ .885$ for both Richmond and Miscellaneous α. It is high, and the fact that the environmental opportunities are different in the two samplings makes no difference. The partial $r_{CA-H.MA}$ is near o for both Richmond and Miscellaneous α.[2]

The total correlations are included, and show the tendencies that have just been discussed. Though they may be used as a sort of common-sense check on what has been said, they could not have been used as a substitute for the partials. The regression equations are very helpful in interpreting the partials mentioned above, but it was not considered necessary to call attention to them in connection with each partial. For a complete set of regression equations, see Table XIV.

Thus it seems that our figures support the extended hypothesis. It is not claimed that we have as many facts bearing upon the matter as would be desirable, but we can say that none of our facts are inconsistent with the hypothesis. The sampling based on 100 cases of grades three and four could not be used here, because one of the four tests upon which M.A. depended was different in these grades. Also one of the sub-tests among the five highest would have been absent. All the figures in support of this hypothesis, then, are based upon 179 pupils of Miscellaneous α and 208 of Richmond. However meager these facts may seem,

[1] The nearer we approach this, the more clear is the meaning of intelligence quotient. If a twelve-year-old child has an M.A. of ten, we say his I.Q. is 83; an eight-year-old child of ten M.A., and I.Q. of 125. But if part of the M.A. of the twelve-year-old child is merely the result of having lived in the world, then is 83 his index of brightness? Likewise, if the eight-year-old child has received a low score on some sub-test or tests, due to physical immaturity or narrow opportunities, and consequently has an M.A. which is too low, how shall we interpret the I.Q. of 125? Further, how shall we compare the 83 and the 125?

[2] Real zero will appear here as a small negative quantity, as has been shown elsewhere (see p. 55), and therefore we are not sure whether the $-.025$ for Richmond or the $-.215$ for Miscellaneous α is the nearer to it. But the important matter is that both approach zero so closely.

the discrepancies between the facts for the two samplings which have been pointed out are worthy of thought. The extent in time to which an individual has lived is of consequence, but the intensity with which he has lived is probably of no less importance in the problem of testing mentality. Extent and quantity have yielded, pretty generally, to mathematical treatment; intensity and quality are not so often subject to numerical study. In this investigation chronological maturity has been handled by statistical means; the other pertinent question as to how rich and varied have been the situations met has been attacked by the method of selection. Of course these two aspects of a child's opportunities are not unrelated, therefore these two have not been mutually exclusive. But light has been thrown on the importance of the twofold problem. The results seem to justify the employing of dissimilar samplings of the population, and give point to the laborious procedure of computing all statistical measures for the groups separately.

CHAPTER VI

SUMMARY AND CONCLUSIONS

1. For the purpose of evaluating sub-tests to determine which depend most on factors irrelevant to brightness it appears that a twofold criterion is necessary. First we need to know how each sub-test correlates with mental age for pupils who are alike in chronological age and environmental circumstances; and second how much each correlates with chronological age for pupils who are alike in mental age. These two aspects of the criterion were handled by the partial correlation technique. A combination of the two was made by a special use of the coefficient of alienation.

2. Three samplings were treated separately. This seems to have been more wise than a plan of treating all cases together, because of the effect of environmental factors.

3. Distinct differences were found among sub-tests when they were submitted to the examination suggested in (1) above. Some of the sub-tests which appeared best for a battery to be used in Grades 5-7 were: 'information', 'sentence completion', 'analogies', 'logical selection'. Some which ranked lowest were: 'visual comparison', 'symbol digit', 'fundamentals of arithmetic', 'picture completion'.

4. By a detailed study of one sub-test it was shown that a component test may be better adapted to the task of measuring intelligence at one level than at another. That is, according to our criterion a sub-test may rank higher over a certain range of mental and chronological age than over another.

5. On the whole, the five sub-tests which rank lowest on the basis of the two formulas, which contained only three variables (viz., sub-test score, M.A., and C.A.), showed a stronger tendency to be affected not only by C.A. but also by environmental factors than did the five highest sub-tests. This point was emphasized strongly because it seemed significant that not only did an older child have advantage over a younger one on some sub-tests of intelligence examinations, but also a child with richer opportunities

had advantage over one whose opportunities were more restricted.

6. To the extent that sub-tests like those that ranked poorest in this study are included in a battery to determine mental age, to that extent is the obtained mental age including some factors that have nothing to do with mental maturity. In order to approach more closely to mental ages which shall not be influenced by differences in opportunities to learn, cannot some practical use be made of the methods and the results of this study along the line of Colvin's suggestion? He said (1921): "I hope the time will soon come when a committee of skilled psychologists will select the elements most valuable in the tests now existing, add others that are lacking, and after carefully standardizing this complete test, will issue it as one recommended for general use in the grades and for the ages for which it has been devised." Those of another school of thought would make a different suggestion. They would say that the whole trend of this study was in support of their contention that the mental age unit is an unsatisfactory one, and that the age-variability unit, by which the mental ability of a subject may be expressed in its relation to the group in which he belongs, is the best means for expressing intelligence ratings. The ultimate conclusions that will be drawn from these results will depend therefore, to some extent, on one's point of view on the whole field of mental measurement; but it is hoped that the findings may prove of some value regardless of whether one is inclined to agree with the mental age method or the age-variability technique of measurement.

If one favors the mental age method it would seem that some technique—the one used here or a better one—should be used to discover sub-tests which are most affected by chronological age and environmental factors, and that such sub-tests should be eliminated so far as it is possible. If this were done, of course new mental ages would result. If one prefers the age-variability method, there may be something of value in the discussion of which sub-tests depend most on environmental factors, and in the fact that some sub-tests are apparently more applicable at one level than at another.

APPENDIX I

AN ANALOGY BETWEEN SCORES ON SUB-TESTS AND DICE THROWS

This section is included for the purpose of showing the calculation of the figures presented on p. 59 and for the purpose of illustrating the points made on p. 62 concerning common elements in correlations.

The case of total for five sub-tests versus total for twenty-six sub-tests.

Let us begin with twenty-six dice. First throw five; count up the total of the throw and let them lie. Call this the x throw. Next throw the twenty-one remaining; count up the total for all dice on the table, that is, the total score for the twenty-six. Call this the y throw. Record in a double entry table the results for a large number of such throws. The correlation would be shown by the formula:[1]

$$r_{xy} = \frac{\text{Number of dice common to } x \text{ and } y}{\text{Geometrical mean of total dice in } x \text{ and } y}$$

$$r_{xy} = \frac{5}{\sqrt{5 \times 26}} = + .439$$

This is a model to which we can, very roughly, fit our problem of comparing a total on five sub-tests with a total on twenty-six sub-tests including the five. Let us consider that each sub-test of the twenty-six may contribute equally to the median M.A. Suppose, for example, that we have twenty-six cubes, each of which has its faces numbered from 3 to 8. Let five of these cubes be green, and the rest white. Throw the green cubes—we'll call them 'dice'—record the total of the throw, and allow them to lie on the table. This is the x throw. Next, throw the remaining 21 and count up the total score of both green and white 'dice.' This is the y throw. Suppose the total of the y throw was 134. Consider it as 134 months' mental age.

[1] Brown and Thomson (1921), *Essentials of Mental Measurement*, p. 141.

The analogy is not perfect, and consequently the results that are obtained are only approximations. The reason why the results are not accurate is that all the assumptions that have been made are not altogether justified by the facts. The assumptions made above are: first, that the score [1] on each sub-test is independent of the scores on all other sub-tests; second, that the variability of the scores on all sub-tests is the same; third, that each sub-test contributes $\frac{1}{26}$ to the composite mental age. This means that we assume that each sub-test can be considered as having a mental age equivalent, and that when we get a summation of the mental age equivalents for all sub-tests—each having been weighted by the fraction $\frac{1}{26}$—we have the mental age. Obviously, this last assumption is at variance with the fact that each of the four group examinations contributed equally (so far as this is possible in case of a median) toward the mental age, regardless of the number of sub-tests in the examination. Since there were five sub-tests in National A, and five in National B, each sub-test contributed roughly $\frac{1}{4} \times \frac{1}{5}$ or $\frac{1}{20}$ toward median mental age. Each of the six sub-tests of Haggerty Delta 2 contributed roughly $\frac{1}{4} \times \frac{1}{6}$, or $\frac{1}{24}$; each of the ten sub-tests of Otis Examination contributed roughly $\frac{1}{4} \times \frac{1}{10}$, or $\frac{1}{40}$ toward the composite. However, the only place where appreciable error would be involved by following the assumption is in the including of sub-tests of the Otis Examination. Since only one Otis sub-test is included in either five highest or five lowest, and since any attempt at correcting this error—which could not be very large—would bring up several intricate problems of weighting, it was decided to be content with the uncorrected figure. That is, it appeared to the writer that since an approximate figure for the purpose of comparison is all that is desired from this computation, the extra work necessary for accurate calculations would be out of proportion to the value of the increase in accuracy.

Let it be made clear that it is not being claimed that the actual scores obtained on these sub-tests *do,* as a matter of fact, show (1) this independence of one another or of the total, and (2) the same variability. The question here is: What would the co-efficient of correlation be, due merely to the common factors existing between five sub-tests and the total including the five, if such conditions did exist? Any amount by which the actual cor-

[1] In mental age equivalent units, which will be explained later.

relation obtained exceeds the correlation based on these assumptions, indicates roughly the effect due to interrelations.

From this detailed account of the analogy between the scores on the sub-tests and dice throws, it is seen clearly what assumptions are made. Though we find it possible to study, under the assumptions, the relation between five sub-tests and twenty-six sub-tests, the futility of attempting to adapt the mental equivalents to physical measures to these assumptions is obvious. Correlation coefficients will indicate concomitant variation which is due to common elements, but correlation cannot always be interpreted as being due to common factors. Whether we can explain our correlations as due to common factors or not, will depend upon our knowledge of the interrelations existing among the variables entering into the correlated series.

APPENDIX II

BIBLIOGRAPHY

BAILOR, E. M. (1924). *Content and Form in Tests of Intelligence.* Contributions to Education, No. 162, Teachers College, Columbia University, New York.

BICKERSTETH, M. W. (1917). "Application of Mental Tests to Children of Various Ages." *British Journal of Psychology,* Vol. 9, pp. 23-73.

BROWN, WILLIAM AND THOMSON, GODFREY H. (1921). *The Essentials of Mental Measurement.* Cambridge University Press, London.

CHAPMAN, J. C. AND DALE, A. B. (1922). "A Further Criterion for the Selection of Mental Test Elements." *Journal of Educational Psychology,* Vol. 13, pp. 267-76.

CHOTZEN, F. (1912). "Die Intelligenzprüfungsmethod von Binet-Simon bei schwachsinnigen Kindern." *Zeitschrift für Angew. Psychologie,* Vol. 6, pp. 411-494.

CLAPAREDE, M. E. (1914). "Tests de Developpement et Tests d'Aptitudes." *Archives de Psychologie,* Vol. 14, pp. 191-197.

COLVIN, S. S. (1921). "Intelligence and Its Measurement. A Symposium." *Journal of Educational Psychology,* Vol. 12, pp. 136-39.

GATES, A. I. (1922). "The Correlations of Achievement in School Subjects with Intelligence Tests and Other Variables." *Journal of Educational Psychology,* Vol. 13, pp. 223-35.

GATES, A. I. AND LA SALLE, J. (1923). "Relative Predictive Values of Certain Intelligence and Educational Tests Together with a Study of the Effect of Educational Achievement upon Intelligence Test Scores." *Journal of Educational Psychology,* Vol. 14, pp. 517-37.

GORDON, HUGH (1923). "Mental and Scholastic Tests Among Retarded Children." Bulletin No. 44, Board of Education Pamphlets, London.

JONES, VERNON A. (1925). "A Study of Children's Abilities to Note Similarities and Differences." *Journal of Educational Psychology,* Vol. 16, pp. 253-60.

KELLEY, T. L. (1923). *Statistical Method.* Macmillan, New York.

KELLEY, T. L. AND TERMAN, L. M. (1921). "Dr. Ruml's Criticism of Mental Test Methods." *Journal of Philosophy,* Vol. 18, pp. 459-65.

MEUMANN, E. (1913). *Vorlesungen.* Engelmann, Leipzig. The part translated by Terman, L. M. (1914). *Journal of Psycho-Asthenics,* Vol. 19, pp. 74-94.

OTIS, A. S. (1922). *Directions: Otis Correlation Chart.* World Book Co., Yonkers, N. Y.

OTIS, A. S. (1923). "The Otis Correlation Chart." *Journal of Educational Research,* Vol. 8, pp. 440-48.

OTIS, A. S. (1925). *Statistical Method in Educational Measurement.* World Book Co., Yonkers, N. Y.

PINTNER, RUDOLF (1923). *Intelligence Testing.* Henry Holt and Co., New York.

PINTNER, RUDOLF AND PATTERSON, D. G. (1914). "Experience and the Binet-Simon Tests." *Psychological Clinic,* Vol. 8, pp. 197-200.

ROOT, W. T. (1922). "Correlations Between Binet Tests and Group Tests." *Journal of Educational Psychology,* Vol. 13, pp. 286-92.

RUGG, H. O. (1917). *Statistical Method Applied to Education.* Houghton Mifflin Co., Boston.

RUML, B. (1920). "The Need for an Examination of Certain Hypotheses in Mental Tests." *Journal of Philosophy, Psychology, and Scientific Methods,* Vol. 17, pp. 57-61.

RUML, B. (1921). "Intelligence and Its Measurement: A Symposium." *Journal of Educational Psychology,* Vol. 12, pp. 143-144.

STENQUIST, J. L. (1921). "Unreliability of Individual Scores in Mental Measurement." *Journal of Educational Research,* Vol. 4, pp. 347-54.

STENQUIST, J. L. (1922). *Manual for Stenquist Tests of Mechanical Aptitude,* p. 3. World Book Co., Yonkers, N. Y.

STERN, WILLIAM (1912). "The Psychological Method of Testing Intelligence." Translated by Whipple, G. M. (1914). *Educational Psychology Monograph,* No. 13.

TAYLOR, GRACE A. (1923). *Inventory of the Minds of Individuals of Six and Seven Years Mental Age.* Teachers College, Contribution to Education, Columbia University, N. Y.

TERMAN, L. M. AND CHILDS, H. G. (1912). "A Tentative Revision and Extension of the Binet-Simon Measuring Scale of Intelligence." *Journal of Educational Psychology,* Vol. 3, pp. 61-74.

U. S. DEPARTMENT OF INTERIOR (1920). *Fourteenth Census of the United States. Population: Occupations.* Washington, D. C.

U. S. *Census* (1920), Vol. 3, p. 856.

WHIPPLE, G. M. (1924). "Endowment, Maturity, and Training as Factors in Intelligence Scores." *Scientific Monthly,* Vol. 18, pp. 496-507.

YERKES, R. M. (1917). "The Binet Versus the Point Scale Method of Measuring Intelligence." *Journal of Applied Psychology,* Vol. 1, pp. 111-22.

YULE, G. U. (1922). *An Introduction to the Theory of Statistics.* Charles Griffin & Co., Ltd., London.